INSIGHT ◉ GUIDES

EXPLORE

TORONTO

⊙ Walking Eye App

YOUR FREE EBOOK AVAILABLE THROUGH THE WALKING EYE APP

Your guide now includes a free eBook to your chosen destination, for the same great price as before. Simply download the Walking Eye App from the App Store or Google Play to access your free eBook.

HOW THE WALKING EYE APP WORKS

Through the Walking Eye App, you can purchase a range of eBooks and destination content. However, when you buy this book, you can download the corresponding eBook for free. Just see below in the grey panel where to find your free content and then scan the QR code at the bottom of this page.

Destinations: Download essential destination content featuring recommended sights and attractions, restaurants, hotels and an A–Z of practical information, all available for purchase.

Ships: Interested in ship reviews? Find independent reviews of river and ocean ships in this section, all available for purchase.

eBooks: You can download your free accompanying digital version of this guide here. You will also find a whole range of other eBooks, all available for purchase.

Free access to travel-related blog articles about different destinations, updated on a daily basis.

HOW THE EBOOKS WORK

The eBooks are provided in EPUB file format. Please note that you will need an eBook reader installed on your device to open the file. Many devices come with this as standard, but you may still need to install one manually from Google Play.

The eBook content is identical to the content in the printed guide.

HOW TO DOWNLOAD THE WALKING EYE APP

1. Download the Walking Eye App from the App Store or Google Play.
2. Open the app and select the scanning function from the main menu.
3. Scan the QR code on this page – you will then be asked a security question to verify ownership of the book.
4. Once this has been verified, you will see your eBook in the purchased ebook section, where you will be able to download it.

Other destination apps and eBooks are available for purchase separately or are free with the purchase of the Insight Guide book.

CONTENTS

FAMILIES

There's no shortage of family fun in Toronto, and first on the itinerary should be Ripley's Aquarium of Canada (route 10), while adventures are sure to be had at the Toronto Zoo (route 12), too.

RECOMMENDED ROUTES FOR...

FOODIES

Savor inexpensive Caribbean jerk chicken in Kensington Market (route 6), authentic Portuguese custard tarts at the St Lawrence Market (route 3), or the finest Canadian specialties at the Richmond Station restaurant (route 1).

HISTORY BUFFS

Discover secret tunnels at Toronto's only castle, Casa Loma (route 9), poke around the historic Spadina Museum (route 9) next door, or learn about Toronto's early origins at the site of Fort York (route 8).

MUSIC LOVERS

With one of the most dynamic music scenes in the country, Toronto has fantastic venues for hosting live performances, such as the renowned subterranean Drake Underground (route 8).

RAINY DAYS

Explore natural history exhibits at the Royal Ontario Museum (route 1), admire Canadian paintings at the Art Gallery of Ontario (route 6), or relish in the tropical warmth of the Allan Gardens Conservatory (route 10).

SHOPPING

Chinatown (route 6) is full of exotic trinket stalls, King Street (route 3) is lined with art galleries, and the CF Toronto Eaton Centre (route 1) is a massive shopping mall with certainly something for everyone.

SPORTY TYPES

Catch an exciting live hockey game (route 11), spend a leisurely afternoon watching the local baseball team (route 11), or have some competitive fun at the Hockey Hall of Fame (route 3).

VIEWS

Standing as a proud beacon, the iconic CN Tower (route 3) offers views from the top that are simply astonishing. For an equally memorable cityscape, head out on a scenic ferry trip to the Toronto Islands (route 7) for the day.

#xoTO

INTRODUCTION

An introduction to Toronto's geography, customs, and culture, plus illuminating background information on cuisine, history, and what to do when you're there.

St Lawrence Market, the city's best food and drink market

EXPLORE TORONTO

As Canada's largest city and the capital of the province of Ontario, Toronto is the epicenter of the country's arts and finance sectors. This ethnically diverse metropolis is also a hub of culture, showcased by its incredible food scene and year-round festivals.

Located along the northwestern shore of Lake Ontario, Toronto sits in a strategic location at the convergence of several key portage and trading routes. No wonder it was crowned capital early on, during the 18th century, of what was then called the province of Upper Canada. A constant influx of new residents from around the globe continued to migrate to this area throughout the 19th and 20th centuries, contributing to the making of what is now one of the most cosmopolitan cities in the world.

GEOGRAPHY AND LAYOUT

With a downtown core of soaring skyscrapers, dwarfed only by the free-standing, iconic CN Tower, the city radiates in all directions, aside from its wide lakeshore edge to the south. The CN Tower is visible from almost anywhere in the city, unless it's a particularly cloudy day, while Lake Ontario is always south, no matter where you are.

Toronto, like most major North American cities, is made up of the downtown core, or City Centre, surrounded by a patchwork of neighborhoods. What's different here though, is that Toronto-

nians don't just work Downtown. They eat, play, and sleep there, too, making Downtown a lively center full of restaurants, cafés, bars, stores, theaters, parks, galleries, and places of worship.

Easily walkable, the City Centre, bounded by Bloor Street to the north, is undoubtedly the heart of Toronto. Many of the city's main attractions are clustered here, including the Art Gallery of Ontario, the Royal Ontario Museum, the Kensington Market neighborhood, Chinatown, the CN Tower, Ripley's Aquarium, the CF Toronto Eaton Centre, the St Lawrence Market, the Distillery Historic District, the Hockey Hall of Fame, and three major sports stadiums.

Streetcars, taxis, and the subway help keep these and other sights close by when it becomes too much on foot. There's even the option of cycling around the city on dedicated bike lanes and utilizing the convenient local bike-share program (see page 15).

The routes in this guidebook will begin in the City Centre, covering the most recommended attractions and highlighting some of Toronto's best neighborhoods including the Waterfront, the Toronto Islands, Kensington

The Toronto Music Garden, themed on Bach's Suite No.1 for Unaccompanied Cello

Market, Chinatown, Little Italy, and The Annex. Finally, several routes will cover worthwhile destinations outside of the city, including the Toronto Zoo, Niagara Falls, and the Niagara Wine Region.

HISTORY

From a provincial backwater to the most prosperous center of the country, Toronto has seen its share of turbulent times, but it was also a beacon of hope for new immigrants right from its humble beginnings.

First Nations began inhabiting the shores along Lake Ontario approximately 10,000 years ago, favoring the area for its rich fishing and hunting grounds, and easily accessible water routes. Over the millennia, these indigenous societies continued to thrive, having no European contact until the 1530s, when French explorer Jacques Cartier journeyed up to the edge of the Great Lakes. Cartier made first but limited contact with what where known as the Iroquois peoples.

Almost a century later, in 1615, French fur trader Étienne Brûlé travelled the Toronto Trail between the lower and upper Great Lakes. He spent some months with indigenous tribes in the area, including the Algonquin.

It wasn't until the 1720s however, that the French began setting up permanent fur trading posts in the area, claiming the territory for France. By the 1750s, the French could not compete with the successful rise of the nearby and competing British traders, and thus they abandoned the posts. British claims for the area were further established as the Seven Years' War came to an end in 1763, officially passing these lands from French to British rule.

British settlers remained and began to farm what was now part of the Upper Canada colony, and it was increasingly under threat by the US to the south. In 1793, British Lieutenant Governor John Graves Simcoe saw an opportunity for the strategically located area to be his new naval base, he named it York, and it became the new capital for Upper Canada. Simcoe was also responsible for developing the town's first two main roads during that time – Dundas Street and Yonge Street.

In 1797, Simcoe had the garrison of Fort York built to protect the new and fast growing town, but by 1812 the US declared war on Great Britain and sought to conquer all of British North Amer-

Toronto's nicknames

Some of the city's more common nicknames are: The Six (referring to the original municipalities of the former City of Toronto, North York, Scarborough, York, Etobicoke, and East York, which joined into one in 1998); T.O. (T for Toronto and O for Ontario); and Hogtown (during the 1890s Toronto had the reputation of having the best bacon and pork manufacturers in the British Empire, or was it the thriving banks during that time that led to this particular nickname…?).

The Art Gallery of Ontario, on the threshold of Chinatown

ica, subsequently attacking Fort York in 1813. The US suffered more casualties than the British and retreated after six days, but only after pillaging and torching much of the fledgling town. These acts led to the retaliatory burning of the White House and other government buildings in Washington by the British in 1814.

York recovered from its invasions and its population began to grow as waves of British immigrants sought out better opportunities in the New World after reeling from the Napoleonic Wars that ended in 1815. In 1834, York was officially incorporated and renamed Toronto, and it continued to prosper as infrastructure improved.

The Great Toronto Fire of 1904 again destroyed much of the town, but it was quickly rebuilt. Toronto was now heavily into manufacturing and excelling in financial services. Banks made huge profits from financing the farming, lumber, and mining industries that were now widespread across the country. From the turn of the 19th century to the late 1920s, Toronto built grand and elegant structures reflecting this, and arts and culture thrived.

Another major development era occurred during the 1960s and 1970s, as immigration restrictions were eased after World War II, and Toronto's liveable Downtown continued to be a draw. Tall new skyscrapers and daring monuments began to fill up the downtown core. In 1976, the city's favorite structure, the CN Tower, was completed and remained the world's tallest free-standing tower until 2007.

Today, Toronto is a large and complex urban center that continues to flourish, rich in culture and prosperous in its economy, retaining its proud heritage as an exciting, welcoming metropolis.

CLIMATE

Toronto's climate is mild by Canadian standards, thanks to the regulating properties of Lake Ontario, though it enjoys all four seasons distinctively, with autumn in particular being a great time to visit. It is then that the trees are ablaze in vivid reds, oranges, and yellows. The temperature, averaging at about 20C (68F), is fresh and comfortable with little precipitation during this time, and the cultural scene is at its best with dozens of festivals celebrating the city's famed multiculturalism.

Early winter is pleasant also, as the city is lit up for the holidays and the snow adds to the cosy atmosphere. In spring, the city is in full bloom but expect more rain and average temperatures of 15C (59F). Summers can be quite humid and hot, reaching easily into the high 20s C (80s F) but relief can always be found in the numerous shady parks and plazas around the city.

POPULATION

Growing on average by 40,000 people every year, the Greater Toronto Area (GTA) currently has a population of 6 mil-

Impressive Niagara Falls

lion. The city alone has over 2,730,000 residents, making Toronto the largest city in Canada, and the fourth-largest city in North America by population.

Diversity Our Strength is Toronto's official motto. With more than half of its 6 million residents originally born outside of the country, the influence of Toronto's

DON'T LEAVE TORONTO WITHOUT...

Indulging at the St Lawrence Market. For the ultimate, market-style grocery shopping experience, this is where Torontonians stock up on cheeses, sweet pastries, fresh seasonal produce, and imported specialties. Try the peameal bacon sandwich from the Carousel Bakery for a delicious, iconic local experience. See page 39.

Drinking a beer in the Distillery Historic District. Local craft breweries abound in Toronto, but a refreshing brew is especially enjoyed in this reclaimed, cobblestoned, pedestrian-only neighborhood where the Victorian architecture blends magnificently with contemporary industrial design. The seasonal Christmas Market here is also memorable. See page 43.

Heading to the top of the CN Tower. Toronto's icon offers a truly unforgettable vantage point from its 446.5-meter (1,465ft) -high floor. Try it at night for an alternative perspective or dare to go out along the thrilling EdgeWalk. See page 37.

Strolling through quirky Kensington Market. Poking around independent boutiques, inviting sidewalk cafés, and cutting-edge art galleries amongst the pretty Victorian-era homes is only surpassed by the plethora of incredible, and affordable, lunch options available in this counter-culture World Heritage Site neighborhood. See page 53.

Feeling the buzz at a live hockey or baseball game. During the winter months, cheer on the Toronto Maple Leafs along with the locals at the Scotiabank Arena. Come springtime, watch the Toronto Blue Jays in the open-air Rogers Centre stadium. At the very least, check out the Hockey Hall of Fame at anytime of year. See page 70.

Exploring the Toronto Islands by bike. Just a short and scenic ferry ride on the lake are a small chain of car-free islands away from the hustle and bustle of the big city. Stroll or bike around peaceful communities and enjoy a picnic along with the wide views from the beach. See page 56.

Admiring the art of the masters. Among Toronto's many excellent museums and art galleries, the Art Gallery of Ontario is a must-see. See page 50.

Feeling the mist of the mighty Niagara Falls. Just 1h30 away from the city, this world-famous natural wonder is worth the trip out. View it during the evening for a magical illumination. See page 78.

Listening to live music at the Drake Underground. This subterranean music venue is one of the hottest in the city and appeals to music fans of all kinds. Join the locals who flock here to catch local up-and-coming acts or see big-name performers. See page 103.

Chinatown signs

200-plus ethnicities is wonderfully obvious in its cuisine, festivals, and dynamic neighborhoods. From Koreatown, Chinatown, and Greektown, to Little Italy, Little Portugal, Little Jamaica, and Little India, the city is vibrating with global diversity, and all seem to blend harmoniously with one another. Even the city's 911 emergency services are equipped to respond in over 150 unique languages.

LOCAL CUSTOMS

Year-round festivals (see page 111) are a big deal in Toronto, as its friendly, global citizens are eager to share their music, traditions, food, and crafts. On the more serious side of things, the city is also the main financial center of the country and thus has a strong work ethic. Come late Friday afternoon, however, and the city's suits begin to unwind at the local bars and bistros.

Toronto may appear to be all business and no pleasure at times, with locals presenting themselves as friendly but not necessarily all that warm and welcoming. It's only due to the anticipated language barriers that Torontonians are accustomed to, given their multicultural city background. Most visitors will find the locals easily approachable once the ice has been broken, so to speak. Good conversation starters could be anything related to the weather, hockey, and where the best poutine – a classic Canadian dish of fries, cheese curds, and gravy – can be found.

POLITICS AND ECONOMICS

As Canada's most populous city, the support of Toronto's voting residents for both federal and provincial elections is undoubtedly crucial. Typically, the city as a whole leans toward the left, favoring both the New Democratic Party and the Liberal Party – two of Canada's current far-left and left, respectively, political parties.

These days however, political discussions are more focused on the American neighbors due south, rather than on local issues. Though plenty of the city's residents are still concerned about the contentious climb of the local real estate market and the nuisance of constant high-rise construction.

As Canada's largest contributor to the economy, at 20 percent of the national GDP, the pressure for success and continued growth of the finance, tech, and tourism sectors, but also the entertainment and manufacturing industries, is noticeable and ongoing.

In the same entrepreneurial spirit, Toronto's eastside is poised to be transformed into a brand new tech town developed by Sidewalk Labs, an Alphabet Inc. company, itself a parent company of Google. The plan is to develop 5 hectares (12 acres) of the city's southeastern waterfront currently occupied by just a few industrial buildings and empty parking lots. Google will build a new headquarters in this potentially car-free zone, as well as residential, office, and commercial space, all using the latest

Pride Toronto is held every year in June

information technology and energy systems, making it essentially a test bed for the giant technology company.

On the surface, Toronto is an ambitious city full of determined people who revel in its fast-paced lifestyle in amongst the soaring concrete landscape. Dig a little deeper however, and visitors will begin to see past the seriousness of its locals and the city as a whole.

Friendly and characterful neighborhoods offer welcoming sidewalk cafés, amazing ethnic restaurants, and independent trendy boutiques. Top-notch music venues, fantastic museums, and striking architecture, both old and new, keep things buzzing. And with its safe, walkable, tree-lined streets, Toronto is an exciting, world-class city to be enjoyed by everyone, no matter the weather.

TOP TIPS FOR VISITING TORONTO

Winter visitors. If you're arriving during the winter months, expect that it can get to sub-zero temperatures, so pack a warm coat and snow boots. To get away from the cool weather, use PATH – a large network of underground tunnels, mostly pedestrian, that connect tourist attractions, such as the CN Tower, with subway stations, shopping centers, and hotels.

Friendly locals. Torontonians can be perceived as a bit icy at first, but it's really just people being busy, and perhaps not even sharing the same language as you as over half of the city's residents have come from outside of Canada. With the Toronto Greeters Program, you can request a free friendly local volunteer to show you around town. Book at www.toronto.ca.

Orientation. Toronto's streets are laid out in a grid, with roads going north and south, and west and east. Most locals will refer to the street names by the first name, for example, King Street East or West will be called just King.

On your bike. Public bikes are available at docking stations around the city and can be borrowed for short to long periods of time for a reasonable fee via the Toronto Bike Share initiative (www.bikesharetoronto.com).

Save time and money. The CityPASS includes admission to the CN Tower, Casa Loma, the Royal Ontario Museum, Ripley's Aquarium of Canada, and either the Toronto Zoo or the Ontario Science Centre, saving you approximately 38 percent, plus you can bypass most ticket lines. It can be purchased online at www.citypass.com or at the participating attractions.

Festivals in the city. Toronto is known for its great year-round festivals (see page 111). Film, music, food, lifestyle, sports, and much more are celebrated with lively events so check the calendar to make sure you catch one while you're in town.

Sales tax and tipping etiquette. Expect a 13 percent sales tax on most retail purchases, plus an extra 4 percent on accommodations. When tipping at a restaurant, plan on 15 to 20 percent if the service was more than satisfactory.

St Lawrence Market sells a variety of fresh produce

FOOD AND DRINK

Toronto's multicultural residents have brought wonderful diversity to the city's food scene. From authentic Chilean empanadas to Singaporean rice noodle soup, the variety of cuisines is endless, with a bit of everything in between.

Top chefs from all over the world are drawn to Toronto's ever evolving and eclectic food scene, with new restaurants popping up weekly. Locally sourced, natural ingredients, including meats and fresh produce, are key to most of the menus presented in the city, and a wide range of prices will suit all budgets.

LOCAL CUISINE

Besides the gravy-and-cheese-curds-covered fries dish called poutine, and the occasional maple syrup-infused offering, Canadian cuisine doesn't have a typical style that can easily be pinpointed. This is probably due to Canada, and especially Toronto, being home to such a diverse group of residents, many of whom have brought their culinary experiences with them.

On any given day in Toronto, hungry patrons are treated to a choice of meals that can include anything from a Cuban sandwich served out of a food truck Downtown, to a Korean rice bowl from an eatery in Koreatown, to the finest Portuguese seafood stew in Little Portugal.

Italian pizzas, Japanese sushi, and Mexican tacos feature too, as do American-style steaks, Chinese dim sum, Indian curries, and Greek lamb dishes.

Although the range of flavors is wide, the communal ethos in Toronto's food scene is to use the freshest ingredients possible, many of which are sourced within a few hundred kilometers from the city. Sustainable and organic seafood, meats, and produce are of great importance to Toronto chefs in creating a menu, as is creativity, and a sense of adventure.

Of course, the typical burger, sandwich or pasta dish is widely available, and vegetarians and vegans will have no problem finding something tasty. Gluten and dairy-free options are often offered as well, as are smaller sized kids meals.

Brunch is a big deal throughout the country and it's no different in Toronto. Often available on weekends only, from the hours of about 10am until 2pm, this in-between breakfast and lunch meal is meant to be enjoyed slowly, ideally accompanied by good friends. Eggs Benedict is the most popular dish, after which the choice of breakfast foods mingled with lunch items is endless. Toronto's oldest restaurant, The Senator (see page 95), with origins dating back to 1836, is a classic diner choice for brunch in the city.

Eggs Benedict brunch at The Senator

Desserts are certainly not an afterthought in Toronto, and can be indulged in at any time of day. From flaky French chocolate croissants and colorful macarons to still-hot-from-the oven donuts, to artisanal ice cream and over-the-top decorated cupcakes, anyone's sweet tooth is well rewarded. Handcrafted chocolates and thick milkshakes are also big hits with Torontonians.

Drinks too, come in both classic and highly creative forms, from single-origin organic coffees to Asian bubble teas, herb-infused specialty cocktails, and locally brewed craft beers. With Canada's largest wine-growing region, the Niagara Peninsula, only a few hours away, local wine is showcased heavily in the city.

WHERE TO EAT

Whether you're an adventurous, multi-course fine diner or simply looking for a quick budget-friendly bite, Toronto's food trucks, innovative bistros, and top-notch restaurants serve up everything from vegan-friendly organic avocado toast to the juiciest local steak on offer.

BUDGET

To start, however, Toronto's iconic food item has got to be the peameal bacon sandwich from the Carousel Bakery (see page 40) in the St Lawrence Market. Simple but delicious, and a must try for any visitor, it consists of a soft white bun filled with mustard-topped, Toronto-invented cured bacon made from pork loin, which is rolled in cornmeal, making it perfectly crispy.

Many other delicious and budget-friendly eats can be found at the St Lawrence Market, including the Lobster Rolls or the Boston Blue Fish & Chips from Buster's Sea Cove (see

Farmers' markets

Adding to the already exciting food scene, Toronto's farmers' markets offer a chance to meet local farmers and artisans, mix with locals shopping for their weekly groceries, and be entertained by live music and performers. Food trucks also feature.
Trinity Bellwoods Farmers' Market; 790 Queen Street West; May–Oct, Tue 3–7pm.
John Street Farmers' Market; 197 John Street; June–Oct, Wed 3.30–7pm.
Nathan Phillips Square Farmers' Market; 100 Queen Street West; June–Oct Wed 8am–2pm.
David Pecaut Square Market; 55 John Street; June–Oct Thu 8am–2.30pm.
Evergreen Brick Works Farmers' Market; 550 Bayview Avenue; year-round Sat 8am–1pm (9am–1pm in winter).
The Junction Farmers' Market; 2960 Dundas Street West; spring–fall Sat 9am–1pm.
St Lawrence Farmers' Market; 93 Front Street East; year-round Sat 5am–3pm.
The Distillery Historic District Sunday Market; 55 Mill Street; June–Oct Sun noon–5pm.

Enjoy dim sum in Chinatown

page 100), the vegan-friendly vegetable-filled Green Wraps from Cruda Café (see page 100), the Polish pierogies from European Delight (see page 100), and, for dessert, the Portuguese custard tarts from Churrasco's (see page 100).

Food trucks are another great option for getting a cheap and cheerful meal, with a choice ranging from soups and sandwiches to tacos and grilled meats, and so much more. Food trucks tend to move around and are scattered throughout the city, but a few hotspots are at the intersection of University Avenue and College Street, and the intersection of Church and Bloor streets. Or check the www.torontofoodtrucks.ca for current and upcoming locations.

The multicultural neighborhood of Kensington Market is filled with affordable places to eat, from Caribbean fare at Rasta Pasta (see page 55) to Mexican tacos from Seven Lives (see page 55), Chilean empanadas from Jumbo Empanadas (see page 93), and buckwheat crêpes from the Hibiscus Café (see page 93).

Koreatown and Chinatown offer some excellent, good-value dining options, including authentic bibimbap rice bowls and dim sum, respectively, as does The Annex district with its plentiful sandwich shops and cheap pub fare due to the large student population living there.

For Canadiana on a budget, try the bagels from Schmaltz Appetizing (see page 65), the frybread tacos from The Pow Wow Café (see page 65) in Kensington Market, or the classic and indulgent poutine from Poutini's House of Poutine (see page 99) Downtown or West Queen West.

MID-RANGE

Along with an often stellar choice of craft beer on tap, the big brew pubs in Toronto are a great choice for a meal anytime of day, even as a late breakfast or brunch option. The Distillery Historic District is home to the ever popular and vast Mill Street Brew Pub (see page 45), or head to Ossington Avenue for the Bellwoods Brewery (see page 102), a local favorite with a lively covered patio. Ossington Avenue is not only a hotspot for pubs and bars, but it's also an area known for its busy, eclectic eateries. The hip Junction district anchored around Dundas Street West and Keele Street is also home to craft breweries, juice cars, organic food stores, bakeries, and vegan restaurants.

Icy souvenirs

Local icewines, such as those from Inniskillin Wines, and dessert wines are prized possessions in Toronto and make excellent gifts to take back home. If you don't get a chance to visit the actual wineries, there are lots of stores that sell them in the city. The LCBO (Liquor Control Board of Ontario, www.lcbo.com) retail stores, with at least five locations just within the downtown core, are a good bet.

Beers at the Bandit Brewery, on Dundas Street

World cuisine in Toronto's restaurants tends to be in the budget to mid-range prices. Neighborhoods such as Little Italy are lined up with excellent pizzerias and trattorias, but there are some great Mexican, Chinese, Korean, and Caribbean options here as well. Likewise, Little Portugal is home to Portuguese restaurants but also several Italian joints, Japanese sushi spots, and Chinese buffet places.

HIGH-END

The downtown core, notably the Financial District, is where fine dining tends to be found. Steakhouses, fine French and Canadian food, and seafood-focused restaurants are common here. Even burgers become high-end in this neighborhood, with a spectacular $40 option from the Bymark (see page 93).

Little Italy too, has its fair share of fine dining options, including the traditional Italian La Palma (see page 98) and the indulgent Spanish tapas Bar Isabel (see page 96).

DRINKS

Craft beer is still having a moment in the city and Toronto currently has over 35 breweries, located all over town, many of them small-batch, micro breweries. One of the most popular is the Bellwoods Brewery (see page 102) over on Ossington Avenue. It produces a variety of barrel-aged craft beers ranging from pale ales to stouts. The award-winning Amsterdam BrewHouse (see page 36) – the city's oldest brewery, going back to 1986 – is known for its flavorful IPAs and smooth lagers.

For classy and creative cocktails, wander around the Entertainment District Downtown for plenty of options, or head to BarChef (see page 102) on Queen Street West – the best of the best for cocktails in the city.

Wine bars in Toronto take things seriously, with an offering of the top wines from the nearby Niagara Peninsula region in addition to Quebecois and British Columbian wines, plus imported varieties. Wines to look out for are the organic Tawse Winery Chardonnays, the Trius Winery blended reds, Inniskillin Wines ice wine, and the Peller Estates Ice Cuvée. Boralia (see page 96) on Ossington Avenue features an impressive local wine list matched in quality by a modern Canadian food menu.

Prefer whiskey or bourbon? Toronto has over a dozen dedicated whiskey bars, with the CC Lounge & Whiskey Bar (see page 103) and The Caledonian (see page 103) boasting the best menus.

Food and Drink Prices

Price for a two-course meal for one including a glass of wine (or other beverage)

$$$$ = over $60
$$$ = $45-60
$$ = $20-45
$ = under $20

High-end shopping in Bloor–Yorkville

SHOPPING

From unique vintage finds to top luxury designer items, Toronto is a shopper's paradise. Familiar global clothing brands are here, as well as locally designed creations and the ubiquitous maple-leaf souvenirs.

WHERE TO SHOP

Mega-mall

Start off at the city's famous CF Toronto Eaton Centre, with more than 250 retailers to browse through. This mega shopping mall, which connects to the underground via PATH (see page 66), includes the flagship location of the Hudson's Bay department store and American luxury department store, Saks Fifth Avenue. Don't forget to look up at the spectacular glass dome galleria inside the mall, where giant Canada Geese sculptures appear to be taking flight.

Luxury

If budget allows, or simply for some fabulous window shopping, the sophisticated Bloor-Yorkville district, known as the Mink Mile, features top sought-after luxury brands including Gucci, Tiffany & Co., Chanel, Louis Vuitton, and the high-end department store Holt Renfrew.

WHAT TO BUY

Local brands

Keep an eye out for local clothing brands Illbury & Goose, Peace Collec-

tive, Pink Tartan, and OVO Clothing, the latter part of local rap artist Drake's record label company.

A Toronto original, Roots, which has three locations within the city, sells women's, men's, and children's casual apparel, most of it featuring their famous Canadian beaver logo. Roots' first store opened on Yonge Street in 1973, just a few blocks north of one of their current store locations.

Another global clothing brand, Canada Goose, though this one specializing in winter gear, also had its humble beginnings in Toronto, back in 1957. Canadian Rangers, local police officers, and film crews working in the city began wearing Canada Goose down-filled parkas during the colder months. Subsequently so did actors and actresses on set, making the brand even more popular. Today, Canada Goose still manufactures its high-quality clothing in Canada, with one of the factories located in Toronto, plus a flagship store on Dufferin Street.

Canadian souvenirs

For memorable souvenirs, the Drake General Store stocks fun Canadiana

Maple syrup fans will be spoilt for choice

items including toques (winter hats), iconic Hudson Bay blankets, and traditional maple syrup. Locally made jewelry, pottery, clothing, and skin care products can be found at any of the three Arts Market locations in the city. The Spacing Store too, has city-themed gift items, as does the gift shop at the Art Gallery of Ontario (see page 50).

Maple syrup doesn't just come in its golden fluid shape, but also in the form of decadent whipped maple butter, lollipop treats, and, at some specialty restaurants, as a maple syrup pie made with a sweet, fudge filling. Savory products too, get their turn with the sweet liquid, such as cured ham, breakfast sausages, and bacon, which are sometimes richly infused with the stuff. Maple syrup in a bottle format comes in various grades and qualities. At the start of the maple syrup season, which generally starts in February, the syrup is lighter and more clear, and it is at this state, at grade A, that it's at its most valuable. Later in the season, the liquid gets darker and darker, and graded a B.

Arts and crafts

Peruse through artists' studios and galleries in the Distillery Historic District, or head to the St Lawrence Market for handmade crafts and delightful edibles. On Sundays, the market fills up even more with dozens of antiques dealers showcasing their unusual wares.

For quirky and novelty items, the Blue Banana Market in Kensington Market is ideal, and while in the neighborhood, browse through secondhand shops, organic produce stores, and indie bookstores. Chinatown is great for exotic trinkets and unusual dried goods.

The 2km (1.2-mile) stretch along Queen Street West, between Bathurst Street and Gladstone Avenue, is known as the Art and Design District. Cutting edge boutiques, menswear stores, and happening cafés and bars line the street here. For a quick respite from shopping, head over to the beautiful Trinity-Bellwoods Park, located about half way along Queen Street West.

Eclectic choice in the Distillery District

Performing at the Beaches International Jazz Festival

ENTERTAINMENT

Toronto's nightlife is alive and kicking with hopping dance clubs, big-ticket musical performances, top-notch theater productions, and lively watering holes. Major venues host the biggest acts, while more intimate bars feature fantastic up-and-coming talent.

The city's nightlife scene is as varied as its neighborhoods. The aptly named Entertainment District Downtown is full of pubs and cocktail bars, catering to the financial sector and after-work crowd, and are therefore at its busiest during the week.

Ossington Avenue, just west of Downtown, is home to some of the city's favorite bars, including The Dakota Tavern (see page 103), a saloon-style hotspot with a variety of nightly music acts. Adjacent Dundas Street West, too, has its fair share of popular local watering holes.

Queen Street West is lined with lively bars, speakeasies, and gastropubs, and some of the city's best live music venues – The Horseshoe Tavern (see page 103) and the Drake Underground, part of the hip Drake Hotel (see page 103).

Drinking tips

The legal drinking age in Ontario is 19. Expect long line-ups at bars and clubs on Friday and Saturday nights anytime after 10pm. While Toronto's liquor laws require bars to stop serving alcohol by 2am, many bars, clubs, and eateries can still remain open until 3, 4, and even 5am.

LGBTQ nightlife centers around Church and Wellesley streets, northeast of Downtown, and The Annex neighborhood is where the majority of students find cheap drinks in dive bars or stay up dancing until 5am at the Coda nightclub (see page 106). And Koreatown is undoubtedly the best location for karaoke bars.

MUSIC AND BALLET

The modern Four Seasons Centre for the Performing Arts (see page 107) is home to the excellent Canadian Opera Company, one of the largest producers of opera in North America. Productions range from classic Mozart and Beethoven, to cutting-edge modern pieces sung in English.

The National Ballet of Canada, the largest in the country and founded in 1951, also performs at the Four Seasons Centre. Traditional and contemporary works are part of the company's repertoire, performed both within Canada and abroad.

To hear the venerable Toronto Symphony Orchestra or the Toronto Mendelssohn Choir, head to the Arthur Erickson-designed, modernist Roy Thomson Hall. While Toronto's Royal Conservatory presents classical, jazz, world, and

Bright lights at the Elgin and Winter Garden theaters

pop music artists at the multi-balcony Koerner Hall, the 1901 Mazzoleni Concert Hall, and the modest Temerity Theatre.

Jazz

Toronto is a haven for jazz enthusiasts. One of the greatest jazz pianists, Oscar Peterson, originally from Montreal, was a local player on the thriving jazz scene in Toronto that began back in the 1940s. Peterson played at the Massey Hall (re-opening in 2020), Roy Thomson Hall, and at some of the jazz festivals. Today, Toronto hosts many other jazz talents too, with dedicated bars (see page 106), the annual TD Toronto Jazz Festival, the Beaches International Jazz Festival, and even attractions such as Casa Loma (see page 63) and Ripley's Aquarium of Canada (see page 66) offering special live jazz evenings.

THEATER

Live theater shows can be seen at the vaudeville-inspired Ed Mirvish Theatre, the Edwardian-era Elgin and Winter Garden theaters (see page 32), the Princes of Wales Theatre (www.mirvish. com/theatres/princess-of-wales-theatre), and the historic Royal Alexandra Theatre (www.mirvish.com/theatres/royal-alexandra-theatre). For stand-up comedy, lots of laughs can be had at The Second City Theatre (see page 106), and for movies, either blockbuster or indie, there are countless movie theaters sprinkled throughout the city.

Special nights out

Various attractions in the city feature a special evening of the week or month where, after hours, the music is turned up, drinks and apples might be offered, and guests can experience something different from the normal day-to-day schedule of the particular venue.

Art Gallery of Ontario. On the first Thursday evening of every month, the AGO presents a late-night event featuring a sneak peek exhibit viewing, live music, talks, and drinks. Check the AGO website (www.ago.ca) for the most current schedule of events.

Royal Ontario Museum. ROM Friday Night Live events are held every Friday night in May and June and include top DJs, artists, drinks and nibbles, plus the opportunity to explore the galleries.

Gardiner Museum. Salon 21 at the Gardiner Museum is a series of musical evenings taking place every third Friday of the month. These are free events and often include food and drinks.

Casa Loma. Throughout the year, this historic castle hosts events that include live jazz, comedy acts, and even murder mystery-type evenings, either in the lush gardens or inside this magical mansion.

Ripley's Aquarium of Canada. Every second Friday of the month, this amazing aquarium features the Friday Night Jazz event where guests can go on guided tours, listen to music, and snack on canapés with a cocktail in hand.

Cycle lane with a view

SPORTS AND OUTDOOR FUN

From a simple stroll along the water's edge in summer to ice-skating in front of City Hall in winter, or catching a live sports game at any time of year, Toronto has a wealth of outdoor activities and sports-related events to keep visitors moving and entertained.

The city is full of interesting walks, such as the waterfront Martin Goodman Trail, ravine hiking trails, and peaceful cycling routes. There are over 855km (530 miles) of bike lanes, off-road paths, and shared roadway routes that make up Toronto's Bikeways Network (www.toronto.ca). Bicycles can be rented from shops around the city and on the bike-friendly, car-free Toronto Islands.

WATERSPORTS

While Lake Ontario isn't so suitable for swimming – it remains icy cold throughout the year and pollution levels can spike quickly, particularly near the city center – watercraft certainly fill up the lake during the warmer months. Kayaks, canoes, and paddle boards can be rented from the Harbourfront Canoe & Kayak Centre to explore hidden lagoons (www.paddletoronto.com). If swimming is still desired, Toronto has 58 seasonal outdoor swimming pools and 60 indoor swimming pools that are open all year (www.toronto.ca).

Beaches
Beachlife is one of Toronto's favorite summer pastimes, and locals flock to the nearby beaches to soak up some sun. Centre Island Beach, Gibraltar Point Beach, Ward's Island Beach, and Hanlan's Point Beach (a clothing-optional one), are some of the best beaches and are all located on the Toronto Islands, just a short ferry ride away.

Cherry Beach, just east of the Toronto Islands at the south end of Cherry Street, doesn't require a ferry ride and is perfect for watching windsurfers at play. The Beaches neighborhood, east of Downtown, has, of course, plenty of lovely beaches, including Kew-Balmy Beach, which features a good concession stand.

Toronto stadiums

Scotiabank Arena (formerly the Air Canada Centre): 40 Bay Street; tel: 416-815-5500; www.scotiabankarena.com
Rogers Centre: 1 Blue Jays Way; tel: 416-341-1000; www.rogerscentre.com
BMO Field: 170 Princes' Boulevard; tel: 416-815-5400; www.bmofield.com
Lamport Stadium: 1155 King Street West; tel: 416-392-1366; www.toronto.ca

Ice-skating in Nathan Phillips Square

ICE-SKATING

During the winter months, there are over 50 outdoor artificial ice-skating rinks that open up throughout the city, all of which will also have skate rentals available. The Nathan Phillips Square in front of City Hall is particularly popular, as is the rink at the Harbourfront Centre, which hosts a DJ night on Saturdays.

GOLF

Golf enthusiasts will find no shortage of greens around, with over 200 golf courses within the Greater Toronto Area alone. Try the legendary 18-hole Don Valley Golf Course in North York, known for its beautiful natural setting, or have a go at the dramatic, Jack Nicklaus-designed Glen Abbey Golf Club in Oakville.

ICE HOCKEY

No visit to Toronto should be without experiencing Canada's favorite sport, ice hockey, whether it's being watched live at the Scotiabank Arena or from a big-screen TV at a buzzing sports bar. Although they haven't won the Stanley Cup since the late 1960s, the National Hockey League's (NHL) Toronto Maple Leafs are still an excellent home team to watch. Catch a live game during the months of October through to April, with free showings on a big, 24-meter screen in Maple Leaf Square or at a dedicated sports bar such as the Real Sports Bar & Grill (see page 72), the Loose Moose, or Wayne Gretzky's. The Hockey Hall of Fame (see page 39) is well worth a visit for sports fans, too.

BALL SPORTS

Canada's professional National Basketball Association (NBA) team are the Toronto Raptors, which also play at the Scotiabank Arena, while Canada's Major League Baseball (MLB) team, the Toronto Blue Jays, plays at the Rogers Centre.

For soccer fans, the Toronto FC soccer team, plays at the BMO Field (see page 71), with regular season games running from March to October. Further local sports teams include the Toronto Argonauts football team, the Toronto Rock national lacrosse team, and the Toronto Wolfpack rugby team – the city's newest pro sports team – that plays at the Lamport Stadium during the spring and summer months.

Paddle-boarding around Ward Island

University of Toronto

HISTORY: KEY DATES

Modern-day Toronto traces its roots back to 1720 when the French established it as a fur-trading post, though long before that, First Nations inhabited the area which was known for its strategic location and rich hunting grounds.

THE FIRST CANADIANS

70000 BC – *c*.AD 1000	First arrivals to Canada are proto-Mongolian peoples, followed by several Indian cultures *c*.8000 BC, the Inuit in *c*.6000 BC, and Icelandic Vikings, who establish coastal settlements in Newfoundland and Labrador *c*.AD 1000.

EUROPEAN ARRIVALS

1615	French fur trader Étienne Brûlé became the first European to travel the Toronto Trail between the lower and upper Great Lakes.
1720	The French establish the site as a fur-trading post, known as Fort Toronto.
1793	British Lieutenant Governor John Graves Simcoe names Toronto, then called York, the capital of Upper Canada (modern-day Ontario).
1796	First parliament buildings are built and Yonge Street is developed.
1803	St Lawrence Market, originally known as the Market Square public market, is established.
1813	America declares war on Britain and invades York, looting and destroying much of the fledgling town.
1834	York is renamed Toronto, to distinguish itself from New York, and is officially incorporated as a city with William Lyon Mackenzie as the first mayor.
1841	First gas-powered lamps are installed in the city.
1844	*The Globe* newspaper is established.
1846	First telegram message transmitted in Canada is sent from Toronto to Hamilton.
1847	38,000 Irish immigrants flee from the Great Famine to Toronto.
1849	The University of Toronto is established, known previously as King's College, which was originally founded in 1827.

Horse-drawn streetcar in the 1880s

1858	Toronto Islands are formed when a violent storm disconnects a sandy peninsula from the mainland.
1861	Toronto's first streetcar service begins, pulled by horses.
1883	Toronto's Public Library opens.
1893	Original Union Station opens; at the time, it was the largest train station in Canada.
1894	Neoclassical performing arts theater Massey Hall is completed.
1897	Temple Building opens at Bay and Richmond streets, and was the tallest office building in Canada at that time.
1899	Construction of the Old City Hall, one of the largest buildings in Toronto at that time, is completed, at a cost of more than $2.5 million (equalling approximately $55 million today).

MODERN TIMES

1904	The Great Fire destroys much of Downtown, including over 100 buildings, and claims the life of one person.
1906	Electricity generated from Niagara Falls begins supplying the city of Toronto.
1914	Royal Ontario Museum (ROM) opens to the public.
1921	Toronto's population swells to over 522,000, fueled by a healthy economy in mining, manufacturing, lumber, and hydroelectric power.
1929	The Fairmont Royal York hotel, known then as the Royal York Hotel, opens.
1954	First subway line under Yonge Street opens and is the first rapid transit line in Canada.
1965	New, modernist Toronto City Hall opens, and is still one of the city's most distinctive landmarks.
1976	CN Tower, built for the Canadian National Railway as an observation tower for the railroad switching yard, is completed.
2005	The Boxing Day shooting occurs on Yonge Street, killing one student and injuring six others.
2010	G20 Toronto Summit is held, where world leaders discuss the global economy, despite major protests.
2015	Toronto hosts the Pan American Games.
2018	10 people are killed and 16 are injured during a vehicle-ramming attack. Sidewalk Labs gets the go-ahead for its ambitious redevelopment project set to transform the waterfront into a high-tech hub.

BEST ROUTES

Ripley's Aquarium's Dangerous Lagoon

CITY HIGHLIGHTS

If you only had one day to see the best attractions that Toronto has to offer, this is the tour for you. Catch views from the CN Tower, a splash at Ripley's Aquarium, historic architecture, shopping, and the fascinating Royal Ontario and Gardiner Museums. Plus dining at one of the city's best restaurants, featuring the finest Canadian cuisine.

DISTANCE: 7km (4.3 miles) walking and subway
TIME: Full day
START: CN Tower
END: Richmond Station
POINTS TO NOTE: The Royal Ontario Museum has discounted Friday evenings from July to September, 5.30–8.30pm, that includes access to all the galleries and exhibits, plus a later affair until 10pm that includes drinks, snacks, and live performances. And to save money and time, the CN Tower, Ripley's Aquarium, and the ROM are all part of the CityPASS (see page 108).

Toronto has countless attractions, but in this route a few of the best are compressed into one day, giving visitors a memorable and enjoyable time in the city and a taste for more.

CN TOWER

From the grand columned limestone Beaux-Arts **Union Station ❶**, built in 1926, walking west along Front Street to Lower Simcoe Street, head south on Lower Simcoe Street and you'll see the **CN Tower ❷** (see page 37) on your right – it's hard to miss. The perspective from the top of the tower is dizzying, and if it's a clear day, you may just be able to see Niagara Falls in the distance.

Over 2 million visitors a year head to the top of this famous tower, so expect a fair wait to get up there. A few ways to avoid the heavy traffic is to go early in the morning, or head up at night and admire it all lit up. Or you can make reservations at the tower's **360 The Restaurant**, skipping the line that way and enjoying a slow, rotating view of the whole city and surroundings while dining on fine Canadian cuisine. Visitors looking for more than just a view though should book an **EdgeWalk** experience (see page 38).

RIPLEY'S AQUARIUM OF CANADA

Next door to the CN Tower is **Ripley's Aquarium of Canada ❸** (see page 66), an entertaining stop with over

The vast Eaton Centre

20,000 marine and freshwater specimens from more than 450 species.

Sharks, sea turtles, stingray, jellyfish, and much more are on full display here, with plenty of hands-on activities that the little ones will adore.

THE CITY HALLS

Backtrack to Union Station, then walk north along Bay Street (or take the PATH SkyWalk, hop on subway line 1 – Finch direction – and head north, getting out at Queen Station). From there turn left onto Queen Street West to **Nathan Phillips Square ❹**, where you'll see the Old and New City Halls.

The modern new City Hall from 1965 (see page 41), stands in stark contrast to the old City Hall (see page 43), built in 1889. Both are worth a quick look, even just from the outside, for their admirable and distinctly different architectural styles. In between the city halls, Nathan Phillips Square is a lively gathering place year round, especially in winter when the water feature turns into an ice skating rink. Admire too, the 1965 Henry Moore sculpture here, *Three-Way Piece No. 2*, locally referred to as *The Archer*, standing as a proud beacon to the city's brave acceptance of modern art back in the 1960s when it was a controversial purchase.

ELGIN AND WINTER GARDEN THEATRES

Head back to Queen Station where, opposite, is a cluster of well preserved histor-

Striking architecture at the Royal Ontario Museum

ical buildings, including the **Elgin and Winter Garden Theatres** ❺ (tel: 416-314-3718; www.heritagetrust.on.ca; guided tours Thu 5pm and Sat 11am; charge for tours), built in 1913, which are the last surviving Edwardian stacked theaters in the world. They are still in use. Next door to these theaters is the old **Bank of Toronto building** ❻, from 1905, though it is currently closed to the public. Around the corner is the even older **Massey Hall** ❼, dating back to 1892. A favorite music venue, it is now undergoing major renovations until at least 2020.

CF TORONTO EATON CENTRE

Back onto Yonge Street and a few steps north take you to the **CF Toronto Eaton Centre** ❽ (tel: 416-598-8560; www.cfshops.com; daily, hours vary). This is North America's busiest shopping mall, covering two city blocks, and it has over 250 stores, restaurants, and services spread across four flours. Several department stores, top global clothing brands, and home decor stores will keep shoppers busy here for hours.

Modeled after a galleria in Milan, the vaulted glass ceilings give an airy feel to this vast indoor space. Canadian artist Michael Snow created the flock of fiberglass Canada geese sculpture, called *Flight Stop*, that is suspended from the ceiling. The Urban Eatery food court, located on the main level, has over two dozen fast food-style restaurants to choose from. As does the **Saks Food Hall**, see ❶, located in the bottom level of the Saks Fifth Avenue department store.

DUNDAS SQUARE

Exiting the mall from the northeast corner, you'll come out onto **Dundas Square** ❾, a public square illuminated by large billboard screens and corporate logos, similar in style to New York City's Times Square. Dundas Square is frequently used as a site for festivals and art installations.

ROYAL ONTARIO MUSEUM

Walk north along Yonge Street for more shopping and dining options, turning west on Charles Street West, about 12 blocks north, or take the subway line 1 at the Dundas Station to the Museum Station, stopping at the **Royal Ontario Museum** ❿ (tel: 416-586-8000; www.rom.on.ca; daily 10am–5.30pm).

With a striking, ultramodern addition that seems to spill out onto Bloor Street, the century-old ROM is one of the largest museums in North America, and the largest in Canada, featuring exhibits on art, culture, and natural history. More than six million artifacts make up its fascinating collection, with notable collections of dinosaur fossils, African art, Egyptian treasures, and Art Deco objects, showcased in more than 40 gallery and exhibition spaces.

Budding astronauts may find the meteorite collection in the Earth and

Clay workshop at the Gardiner Museum

Space galleries fascinating, as the ROM is home to the world's largest piece of Springwater pallasite – a rare meteorite discovered in 1931 near Springwater, Saskatchewan, that's 4.5 billion years old and weighs nearly 53kg (117lbs).

As part of the Natural History galleries on the second floor, the simulated Bat Cave is entertaining for the whole family, featuring over 800 wax models of bats in a recreated habitat. Or view extinct species such as the dodo bird or the passenger pigeon.

For a further look into Canadian history, the Canadiana exhibit showcases fine First Nations artifacts including beautiful wooden canoes, intricate leather clothing, and unusual weaponry. There's also a display of works by Paul Kane (1810–71), and Irish-born Canadian painter who's famous paintings and sketches of the First Nations were a valuable resource for ethnologists and are often still used to this day for research purposes.

GARDINER MUSEUM

Across the street from the ROM, on the west side, sits Canada's national ceramics museum, the **Gardiner Museum** ⑪ (tel: 416-586-8080; www.gardinermuseum.on.ca; daily 10am–5pm, Fri until 9pm). It houses a collection of over 4,000 pieces, ranging from earthenware vessels and sculptures from the Americas dating back to 3500 BC, to 16th-century English delftware and modern Canadian pottery. The museum also offers clay workshops

for all ages, and the gift shop is excellent for souvenirs. Guided tours are included with admission and the entry fee is half price Friday early evenings.

To finish off the day, hop back onto line 1 at the Museum Station and get out at Queen Station. Walk south on Yonge Street and west on Richmond Street West to one of the city's top restaurants, **Richmond Station**, see ②.

Food and Drink

① SAKS FOOD HALL

CF Toronto Eaton Centre, Saks Fifth Avenue; tel: 416-365-3130; www.pusateris.com; daily B, L, and D; $
More like a gourmet specialty food store, this is a collection of aisles and mini-restaurants featuring a well-curated assortment of the finest produce, baked goods, sweets, deli meats and cheeses, pantry items, exotic imports, and prepared dishes. There's a Champagne bar, a yogurt bar, a juice bar, and an Italian pizzeria, just to name a few options.

② RICHMOND STATION

1 Richmond Street West; tel: 647-748-1444; www.richmondstation.ca; Mon–Sat L and D; $$$
Seasonal, local, and creative Canadian dishes in a casual atmosphere. The Station Burger is a best seller, but the Duck Two Ways with a parsnip purée or the Rabbit Three Ways with braised bacon and onions are outstanding as well.

Experience a harbor cruise on the Schooner Kajama

A SHORT STROLL ALONG LAKE ONTARIO

For a short and sweet introduction to the city of Toronto, a casual stroll along the lively boardwalk of the Harbourfront Centre is the perfect place to begin.

DISTANCE: 0.5km (0.3 miles) walking
TIME: Half day
START: Harbourfront Centre
END: Amsterdam BrewHouse
POINTS TO NOTE: This is a walking tour, and the Harbourfront Centre is easily reached via the 509 or 510 streetcars, both of which stop in front of the center. From Union Station it's a 15-minute walk south along Lower Simcoe Street or York Street. The PATH network will take you most of the way as well, stopping just east of the center, at the RBC WaterPark Place.

Already visible from most vantage points, and if time permits, the iconic CN Tower (see page 37) is just a 15-minute walk north of the Harbourfront Centre, once again crossing Queen's Quay West. Right next door to the CN Tower is Ripley's Aquarium of Canada (see page 66) and the Rogers Centre (see page 71). Further east, another 10 minutes walking, is the Scotiabank Arena (see page 70). And the ferry terminal to the Toronto Islands (see page 56) is 500 meters/yds to the east.

This route allows for an easy introduction into getting to know the city from the waterfront, before stepping right into it, with a relaxed walk, some interesting art along the way, and a filling lunch over which further touring plans can be discussed and planned out.

HARBOURFRONT CENTRE

Walking south along York Street, crossing Queen's Quay West, or stepping off from the 509 Harbourfront or 510 Spadina streetcars, both of which stop directly in front of the main building of the **Harbourfront Centre** ❶ (tel: 416-973-4000; www.harbourfrontcentre.com; daily 10am–11pm), head west to the Queen's Quay Terminal, then south along the water's edge.

Nestled along the shores of Lake Ontario, directly south of Downtown, the Harbourfront Centre is a 4-hectare (10-acre) waterfront park that was revitalized in the 1970s out of old

The marina at Queen's Quay Terminal

warehouses from the 1920s and is currently undergoing another spruce-up with the opening of new public spaces Canada and Ontario Squares as well as Exhibition Common. The park buzzes year-round with events such as free festivals, big-name concerts, live performances, art installations, and movie screenings.

Theaters, art galleries, cafés, stores, and design studios have a home here in the spacious buildings. The Bill Boyle Artport inside the Harbourfront Centre's main building was transformed from an old trucking garage into an art gallery on the first level. The Artport Gallery, specifically, features ongoing exhibitions of local and global contemporary design, craft, photography, and architecture.

In winter, the Natrel Pond turns into an outdoor skating rink, free for all to use, with evening entertainment on Saturdays by various DJs.

QUEEN'S QUAY TERMINAL

Being mindful of cyclists along the Martin Goodman Trail and Waterfront Trail bike paths, begin your walk from the southeast corner of the boardwalk by the **Queen's Quay Terminal ❷**. Built in 1926, this Art Deco building was originally an old warehouse facility that was later converted into condominiums and a shopping mall complex in the early 1980s. It includes a Sobeys grocery store – a handy stop for picnic items – as well as an array of fast-food eateries.

Note that just 500 meters/yds to the east of Queen's Quay Terminal is the Jack Layton Ferry Terminal, the departure point for foot passengers on one of three ferry routes across to the Toronto Islands (see page 56).

Take in the lake views, admiring the cruise ships, yachts, and sailboats moored along the water's edge here, and enjoy the street performers during the summer months. Inviting cafés and pubs with large, waterside patios, tourist shops, ice cream vendors, and art galleries are all accessible along the way, plus plenty of shady spots to sit and relax.

For a cup of strong coffee accompanied by a freshly baked pastry, stop by the **Boxcar Social**, see ❶, on the

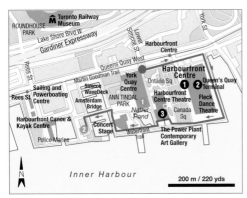

The Power Plant Contemporary Art Gallery

first level of the main Harbourfront Centre building, facing the lake. Or head back here later in the evening for a sweet sundowner out on the waterfront patio.

THE POWER PLANT CONTEMPORARY ART GALLERY

A noteworthy stop is **The Power Plant Contemporary Art Gallery** ❸ (tel: 416-973-4949; www.thepowerplant.org; Tue–Sun 10am–5pm, Thu until 8pm, holiday Mon; free), just south of the Harbourfront Centre Theatre and located right along the boardwalk. Housed in a former powerhouse red-brick building from the 1920s, this cutting-edge gallery is dedicated to presenting the latest Canadian and international artists.

This free gallery doesn't have a permanent collection, rather, it's constantly seeking out and presenting new artistic talents. It also hosts educational programs and public events and publishes art books. There are free 30-minute guided tours on Saturdays starting at 3pm, and free lectures on Sundays revolving around the current exhibit.

AMSTERDAM BREWHOUSE

Next door to The Power Plant is the **Natrel Pond**, which doubles as an ice-skating rink during the winter months. Heading around the corner, passing by the Concert Stage, a small pedestrian bridge takes you across

toward the **Amsterdam BrewHouse**, see ❷. You can't reserve a spot on the patio so be prepared to wait during the warmer months, but it will be well worth it. Sip a cold brew here (ask for a flight selection to try more than one) or some good pub grub and enjoy the view.

Food and Drink

❶ BOXCAR SOCIAL

235 Queens Quay West; tel: 647-349-1210; www.boxcarsocial.ca; B, L, and D daily; $$

Not just a pretty, spacious café, this industrial-feel eatery with a gorgeous lake-view patio offers an Italian-inspired lunch and dinner menu with sandwiches, salads, and snacks to match its excellent and well-curated coffee, craft beer, whiskey, and wine menus.

❷ AMSTERDAM BREWHOUSE

245 Queens Quay West; tel: 416-504-1020; www.amsterdambeer.com; daily 11.30am–11pm, Fri–Sat until 2am; $$
Spacious, lakeside pub with a wide selection of draft, seasonal, and cask offerings. Ask for a tasting flight to sample their beers, or go on a brief brewery tour. Try getting a seat outside on the patio facing the harbor, then pair your drinks with some freshly baked pretzels, their famous buffalo cauliflower appetizer, and a juicy burger.

The CN Tower SkyPod

DOWNTOWN WEST

The CN Tower is on most tourists' itinerary, and for good reason – the views really are spectacular. And from this modern wonder, the tour will take you back to the city's historic boom, an unmistakable fact that's clearly noticeable by the early and imposing architecture.

DISTANCE: 3.2km (2 miles) walking or partly by streetcar
TIME: Full day
START: CN Tower
END: Drake One Fifty
POINTS TO NOTE: The St Lawrence Market is always closed on Mondays and the food vendors are also closed on Sundays, so it may be best to do this tour on any other day as you won't want to miss all the delicious offerings inside. The Cathedral Church of St James is free to enter and has an 18-voice choir that sings at 11am and 4.30pm every Sunday. Pipe organ recitals are at 1pm on Tuesdays and 4pm on Sundays.

Contained within Queen Street West to the north, Front Street West to the south, Yonge Street to the east, and Spadina Avenue to the west, the Downtown West neighborhood contains not only stacks of glimmering glass condos, but also the city's entertainment, fashion, and financial districts. It is where Torontonians work, play, and sleep. In this route we've also included the iconic CN Tower just south of Front Street, and the St Lawrence Market, just to the east.

This route starts at the CN Tower; the closest subway station is Union Station, from there it's a short walk southwest via the PATH tunnel.

CN TOWER

Wherever you may be in the city, the slender concrete structure of the **CN Tower ①** (tel: 416-868-6937; www. cntower.ca; daily 8.30am–11pm) is nearly always visible. Built in 1976 by the Canadian National Railway Company (CN), its original purpose was to act as a TV and radio communication platform for the city, and as a posturing device for the, at that time, powerful CN.

The viewpoint from the 447m (1,465ft) interior SkyPod (equivalent to 147 building stories) has, of course, an even more stunning vantage point. The Observation Deck also boasts a glass floor for those who aren't scared of looking straight down.

Union Station

For an even more thrilling view, literally, book an EdgeWalk experience – the world's highest full circle hands-free walk on a 1.5m (5ft) wide ledge encircling the top of the tower's main pod, 356m (1,168ft) high. Attached to a harness linked to an overhead safety rail you can literally let yourself hang, suspended over the city.

With views of up to 160km (100 miles), reaching as far away as Niagara Falls and New York State, standing at any of the elevated levels of the tower will offer a spectacular experience. This famous Toronto icon is certainly the number one tourist attraction of the city, with over 1.5 million visitors reaching the top levels every year.

For smaller crowds at the tower, arrive before 11am or after 6pm or consider dining at the tower restaurant, **360 The Restaurant**, see ❶, so you can skip the line ups and admission is included with the price of your meal.

FRONT STREET

Exiting east from the CN Tower via the PATH Sky-Walk (see page 66), head toward Union Station on Front Street West. Front Street has a series of impressive buildings from the 1920s, a time in which the city felt highly prosperous and respected.

Exiting out onto Front Street, admire the Beaux-Arts architecture of the limestone **Union Station** building built in 1926. It is the third Union Station, with the first two originally located behind the current station.

Directly across Front Street is the opulent **Fairmont Royal York**, built by the Canadian Pacific Railway in 1929. This site has been operating as a hotel since 1853, and rising to 28 floors, the current château-style hotel was the tallest building in Toronto at that time, even the tallest in the British Empire.

Continuing along Front Street, you'll soon reach another Beaux-Arts style building standing on the south side of the street. This is the **Dominion Public Building**, built in 1926, and it now houses office space for the Canada Revenue Agency.

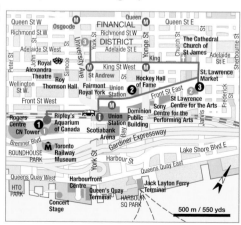

The Hockey Hall of Fame, a tribute to Canada's national obsession

HOCKEY HALL OF FAME

At the intersection of Yonge Street and Front Street East is the **Hockey Hall of Fame ❷** (tel: 416-360-7765; www. hhof.com; Mon–Sat 9.30am–6pm, Sun 10am–6pm), a sports museum dedicated to the history of ice hockey. Inside, visitors can learn about hockey history, see the Stanley Cup, and shoot real pucks, among other interactive games. Not surprisingly, the NHL team with the most player inductees honored at the Hockey Hall of Fame is the local Toronto Maple Leafs, with 64 out of a total of 276 players.

The museum is housed in an impressive former Bank of Montreal head office building from 1885. The ornate facade with intricate carvings, columns, and pediments were meant to evoke a prosperous and secure image of the bank.

Continuing on east on Front Street, passing by the **Sony Centre for the Performing Arts** and the **St Lawrence Centre for the Arts**, the back of the 1892 red-brick flatiron **Gooderham Building** can be seen just after Berczy Park. The large mural is by Canadian artist Derek Michael Besant, using a trompe l'oeil effect.

ST LAWRENCE MARKET

Just ahead one more block, on the south side of Front Street is the historic **St Lawrence Market ❸** (tel: 416-392-7219; www.stlawrencemarket.com; Tue–Sun 8am–6pm) and the perfect spot for a break. Try the peameal bacon sandwich from the **Carousel Bakery**, see ❷. Note that this is a cash-only establishment.

The site of a public market since 1803, the St Lawrence Market is divided into three buildings – South, North, and the Hall. The main and lower levels of the South Market contain over 120 specialty food and craft vendors, featuring fresh and local produce, flowers, meats, seafood, baked goods, prepared foods, and much more.

The North Market is primarily known for its Saturday Farmers' Market where

CN Tower facts

• Guests rocket 58 seconds and 22km/hour (15 miles/hour) upward in one of six glass-fronted elevators to the LookOut Level located at 346m (1,136ft). Some of these elevators have glass floor panels, too.

• The 360 restaurant revolves once every 72 minutes.

• The EdgeWalk is at a height equivalent to 116 building stories.

• The total height of the tower is 553.33m (1,815.5ft), and it was the world's tallest tower, building, and free-standing structure from 1976–2010.

• Today the tower still provides transmission for television, radio, and wireless service providers.

• Most nights the tower is lit up with LED lights according to the occasion, whether it's a special holiday or in honor of someone noteworthy.

Browsing at the St Lawrence Sunday antiques market

Food and Drink

❶ 360 RESTAURANT

301 Front Street West; tel: 416-362-5411;
www.cntower.ca; L and D daily; $$$
At 1,151 feet (351m), dining at this
revolving restaurant at the top of the CN
Tower is an unforgettable experience, and
not just for the incredible views. The fine
Canadian menu has a seafood focus with
Atlantic salmon, cod, and lobster dishes.
The wine list, too, is all Canadian.

❷ CAROUSEL BAKERY

93 Front Street East (Upper Level); tel:
416-363-4247; www.stlawrencemarket.
com; Tue–Sat B and L; $
Home of the famous Canadian peameal
bacon sandwich, this Portuguese bakery
is popular with celebrities, tourists, and
locals alike. On a typical busy Saturday,
an incredible 2,000 of their famous
sandwiches will be sold. Cash only.

❸ DRAKE ONE FIFTY

150 York Street; tel: 416-363-6150;
www.thedrake.ca; daily L and D; $$$
An offshoot from the iconic Drake Hotel
on Queen West Street, this big colorful
brasserie is art-adorned and features
lovely vintage and modern decor, just like
the hotel. The menu is new Canadian,
so you can expect a bit of everything
– salads, tapas, pizzas, seafood, and
burgers, though all refined and upscale.
Cocktails, too, are chic and delicious.

producers from the surrounding area
bring their seasonal goods to the city.
On Sundays, this space is filled with
over 80 antiques dealers. The St Lawrence Hall, north, across the street on
King Street East and built in 1850, is
used as a venue for concerts, exhibitions, and other public events.

KING STREET

Walk north up Jarvis Street after the
St Lawrence Hall, to King Street East.
From here you can choose to continue
walking west along King Street or take
streetcar 504 or 514 to York Street.

If continuing to walk along King Street,
have a look at the exterior of **The Cathedral Church of St James** (tel: 416-
364-7865; www.stjamescathedral.ca;
Sun–Fri 7am–5.30pm, Sat 9am–5pm;
free), just after the shady St James Park
on the north side of the street. The par-
ish for this Anglican church was established in 1797, while construction on
the Gothic Revival-style brick and sandstone cathedral began in 1850.

Art galleries, spas, luxury home decor
stores, cafés, and lively restaurants and
bars line King Street. As you continue
west, the historical architecture makes
way for modern office buildings and condominiums. For dinner, there's a plethora
of choice, depending on your mood and
budget. Our pick is to go north on York
Street where you'll find the artsy **Drake
One Fifty**, see ❸, with its creative Canadiana cuisine and busy streetside patio.

The reflecting pool in Nathan Phillips Square turns into a skating rink in winter

THE HISTORIC HEART

Striking architecture, both contemporary and historic, features in this walking tour, where you'll also find excellent brews, artisan chocolates, local art for sale, and a few good laughs to end the day.

DISTANCE: 3km (1.9 miles) walking or partly by streetcar
TIME: Full day
START: Toronto City Hall
END: Distillery Historic District
POINTS TO NOTE: A free brochure detailing a self-guided tour of the new city hall is available from the information desk inside, or it can be downloaded online (www.toronto.ca). During the winter months, the reflecting pool in the Nathan Phillips Square is used as a skating rink, which is open to the public and free.

Starting at the true heart of the city, this route gives a brief history lesson of Toronto spanning over a century, with plenty of side distractions, if time permits. If you're starting off in the morning and you haven't had breakfast yet, then **Eggspectation**, see ❶, is just what you're looking for before you set out – their Eggs Benedict are delectable.

TORONTO CITY HALL

As you stand in **Nathan Phillips Square**, with the striking modernist **Toronto City Hall** ❶ (tel: 416-397-5000; www.toronto.ca; Mon–Fri 8.30am–4.30pm; free) in the center and historic buildings all around, the sense of this being the heart of the city is clear. Thousands of visitors come to this buzzing space on a daily basis and it's the ideal start to this walking route.

Chosen from an international competition consisting of more than 500 competitors from 42 countries, the new Toronto City Hall was opened in 1965 and immediately became the unique civic symbol that it is to this day.

Just inside the entrance, local artist David Partridge created the mesmerizing sculptural mural *Metropolis* out of more than 100,000 copper and galvanized nails.

The large bronze sculpture in front, *Three-Way Piece No. 2*, but more commonly know as *The Archer*, was created by British artist Henry Moore in 1965.

Toronto's modernist City Hall

It was commissioned to follow the flowing lines of the new city hall structure, and it was a highly controversial piece at the time, considering the cost ($100,000CAD) and its unconventional, abstract shape.

Less than a decade later, this purchase encouraged Moore to bestow hundreds of pieces of his work – sculptures, prints, and drawings – to the Art Gallery of Ontario (see page 50), which now houses the largest public collection of his art in the world.

From the air, the new city hall resembles a giant unblinking eye, earning the nickname 'The Eye of the Government.' A Finnish design, the futuristic concrete structure was built to replace the Old City Hall, the copper-topped Roman-esque-style building with the distinctive clock tower across the street.

Podium Green Roof

Atop City Hall sits a hidden sanctuary: just follow the winding ceremonial ramp that leads from Nathan Phillips Square to the **Podium Green Roof**. Consisting of environmentally-conscious landscaped gardens, this space is open to the public year-round. Wooden benches are scattered around, while a concrete path runs through it. Plants are arranged according to color, ranging from yellows and oranges in the west, to purples and reds in the east. At night, it's the LED lights that provide the gardens with flashes of color.

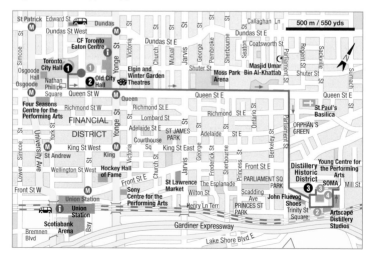

Old City Hall clock

OLD CITY HALL

Designated a National Historic Site, the **Old City Hall** ❷ (tel: 416-338-0338; www.toronto.ca; Mon–Fri 8am–6.30pm; free), built in 1889, is a fine example of Romanesque Revival architecture. At the time of its construction, it was one of the largest buildings in Toronto.

The two-tone sandstone exterior features a 103-meter (340ft) clock tower with four bronze gargoyles near the top, though these gargoyles are replicas since the originals have been lost. Near the building's entrance, several faces are carved in the stone pillars, faces of the political figures and the original architect, E.J. Lennox. Lennox was also the architect for the city's famous faux castle, Casa Loma (see page 63).

Original interior features of the Old City Hall include an impressive staircase, an arcade with murals of early pioneers and angels, intricate stained-glass windows, marble columns, and a mosaic floor. Today, the Old City Hall is used as a courthouse but the building is open to the public during regular business hours. Future plans are to turn the building into a museum of Toronto and public library.

Across Bay Street from both city halls is the huge CF Toronto Eaton Centre shopping complex. If the weather is not cooperating, or you simply feel like some retail therapy, this is the place to go. The food court is decent here as well, if you're feeling peckish.

Beyond the CF Toronto Eaton Centre, on the opposite side of Yonge Street are the Elgin and Winter Garden Theatres, the Bank of Toronto building, and around the corner on Shuter Street, the Massey Hall – all stunning heritage buildings that are certainly worth a look, even from the outside.

DISTILLERY HISTORIC DISTRICT

From the Old City Hall walk east on Queen Street West for about 10 blocks, taking breaks in the parks along the way, or take either the 514 streetcar from King Street three blocks south, or the 501 streetcar eastbound, getting off at Parliament Street. Walk south along Parliament Street, heading into the **Distillery Historic District** ❸ (tel: 416-364-1177; www.thedistillerydistrict.com; Mon–Wed 10am–7pm, Thu–Sat 10am–8pm, Sun 11am–6pm; free), starting at Gristmill Lane, in between Parliament and Mill Street.

A National Historic Site, the whole Victorian-era and fully restored 5-hectare (13-acre) area features 47 brick and stone heritage buildings dating back to as early as 1859, all originally belonging to the Gooderham & Worts Distillery complex – once the world's largest distillery which began with a simple sill in 1837.

The atmospheric Distillery District

Being car-free, pedestrians can wander along the cobbled streets here and peak into the art galleries, design studios, and chic clothing boutiques housed in high-ceiling, converted warehouses and 21st-century modern buildings, at their leisure. Whimsical sculptures are sprinkled throughout the streets, many allowing for perfectly fun photo opportunities.

For those with shopping in mind, head to **Bergo Designs**, at 28 Tank House Lane, with its selection of award-winning, stylish home decor,

Outside Balzac's

unusual watches, and fun Canadiana items. Or try **Blackbird Vintage Finds**, at 55 Mill Street, for a treasure trove of anything from new French soaps to antique American typewriters.

Gristmill Lane

As brick-lined Gristmill Lane narrows, the **John Fluevog Shoes** store is visible on the right. A Vancouver original from the early 1970s, this quirky store sells unique eye candy for both women and men's feet in quality leather and outlandish designs. Gristmill Lane opens up to Trinity Street, filled with larger-than-life public art.

Trinity Street

Trinity Street is home to the main public square and where outdoor markets, festivals, and other events are frequently held. For a relaxing coffee break, grab a seat either outside or inside the cozy, atmospheric **Balzac's**, see ❷. For a more substantial but still casual lunch, try the **Brick Street Bakery**, see ❸.

Case Goods Lane and Tank House Lane

The Case Goods Warehouse and the Cannery Building, just east of the Trinity Street square, is home to dozens of artists' studios, known collectively as the **Artscape Distillery Studios**. Pop into one of the open studios for a glimpse or even a purchase of local artwork.

Celebrating all things Canadian in this Distillery District store

Farther up, on Tank House Lane, is **SOMA** – an exquisite chocolatier located in a former whisky-aging tank-house. Try their truffle chocolates, which come in unusual flavors such as strawberry rhubarb, brown butter, bergamot, douglas fir, magnolia peach, and jasmine. SOMA uses all natural flavorings, locally grown fruit where possible, and both fair-trade and organic cacao beans.

If dinner sounds ideal by now, the **Mill Street Brew Pub**, see ❹, is an easy choice. Followed by a theatrical performance by the Soulpepper Theatre Company at the **Young Centre for the Performing Arts** (tel: 416-866-8666; www.youngcentre.ca; nightly performances except Mon). The Young Centre features a range of high quality live performances, from classic dramas, to satires, fringe, and comedies.

Food and Drink

❶ EGGSPECTATION

483 Bay Street; tel: 416-979-3447; www.eggspectation.com; daily B and L; $
A Montreal original, this small but now global breakfast chain will start your day off right. Begin with a freshly squeezed juice, followed by Belgian waffles topped with strawberries and a salted maple caramel sauce or Eggs Benedict with sautéed Maritime lobster. Sit outside on the patio if you can get a seat there, and watch busy Torontonians heading to work.

❷ BALZAC'S

1 Trinity Street; tel: 416-207-1709; www.balzacs.com; daily B, L, and early D; $
Housed in an 1895 pump house, this two-story Parisian-style café serves excellent organic coffees and accompanying snacks. Pick up a bag of the Atwood Blend freshly roasted coffee beans as a fragrant souvenir to take back home.

❸ BRICK STREET BAKERY

27 Trinity Street; tel: 416-214-4949; www.brickstreetbakery.com; daily B, L, and early D; $
Great little bakery with a few spots to sit inside and outside. The freshly made sandwiches, pastries, and desserts are all made using organic flour, natural meats, and local vegetables. Try the Cornish Pasties and the Sausage Rolls for savory, satisfying goodness.

❹ MILL STREET BREW PUB

21 Tank House Lane; tel: 416-681-0338; www.millstreetbrewery.com; daily L and D, Sat–Sun B; $$
Spacious brewpub that produces an organic lager, refreshing ales, and a bold stout. The elevated pub food menu includes generous portions of various poutines, curries, and burgers. Daily tours of the onsite brewery are available, or sit out on the patio and enjoy plentiful people watching.

Fairmont Royal York hotel

ALONG UNIVERSITY AVENUE

A slice of Toronto, with grand buildings, both historic and modern, spanning nearly 200 years, sprinkled with some art, lush gardens, and delightful dining options.

DISTANCE: 2.5km (1.6 miles) walking
TIME: Half day
START: Union Station
END: Queen's Park
POINTS TO NOTE: Although this is meant as a walking route, there are four subway stations along the way if walking continuously is not an option.

Standing outside of Union Station on Front Street West, University Avenue begins, one of the city's major north–south roads, and it ends just south of Queen's Park. All along the way are interesting city landmarks, pretty boulevards with shady rest spots, and wonderful restaurants, as this route will certainly convey.

TRIAD SCULPTURE

The first stop is on Front Street West, in front of the Citigroup Place building. There stands *Triad* ❶, a 10.5-meter (35ft) sculpture of three, twisting, stainless steel columns. Designed by Canadian sculptor Ted Bieler in 1984, it was commissioned to mark the occasion of Toronto's 150th birthday, symbolizing the growth of the city and the unity of its residents.

FAIRMONT ROYAL YORK

Walking north along University Avenue now, as it branches off of York Street, the noble, copper-topped **Fairmont Royal York** ❷ (see page 85) can be seen to the west along Front Street West. Built in 1929 by the Canadian Pacific Railway, it was constructed on the site of two previous hotels, the first dating back to 1843. As the Royal York in 1929, it was a state-of-the-art hotel at that time, considering that it had ten ornate elevators reaching all 28 floors, each room had a private radio and ensuite bathroom, and there was even a golf course on site. The Royal York was also home to the Imperial Room, one of the city's legendary nightclubs from the 1940s until the 1990s, hosting famous international entertainers including Marlene Dietrich, Peggy Lee,

The Great Library at Osgoode Hall

and Ella Fitzgerald among countless others.

Continuing north, just past Adelaide Street West, on the west side past the Shangri-La Hotel (see page 87) and up inside a glass cube, is the **Momofuku Noodle Bar**, see ❶, an excellent spot for lunch or dinner (the latter likely requiring reservations), specializing in Asian-fusion noodle dishes.

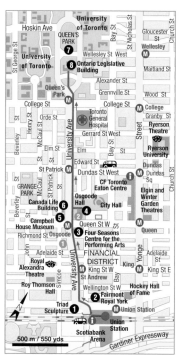

FOUR SEASONS CENTRE FOR THE PERFORMING ARTS

Crossing over to the east side at Richmond Street West, is the modern, glass structure of the **Four Seasons Centre for the Performing Arts** ❸ (see page 107). This 2,071-seat theater, built in 2006, is home to the Canadian Opera Company and the National Ballet of Canada.

The main glass facade has a computer-controlled exterior shade that responds to weather sensors, keeping the interior at comfortable temperatures, even on the hottest of days. The glass staircase inside the Isadore and Rosalie Sharp City Room is one of a kind – it's the longest free-spanning glass staircase in the world.

Major performances take place at the centre, from big-ticket production to chamber pieces and large-scale orchestras. During the months of late September though May, this venue also hosts a Free Concert Series on most Tuesdays and Thursdays at noon.

OSGOODE HALL

Across Queen Street West is the neoclassical **Osgoode Hall** ❹ (Mon–Fri 9am–5pm), surrounded by an ornate wrought-iron fence – that was originally erected to keep cows and horses off its immaculate lawn – and leafy, manicured gardens on a 2.5-hectare (6-acre) property. This landmark building dates

The Canada Life building

from 1832 and originally served as the headquarters for the Law Society of Ontario, and it operated as a law school until 1959. It now houses the Ontario Court of Appeal, and other branches of the court, which are also housed in the modern, 1960s Toronto Courthouse next door.

The old courthouse, the Great Library, and the Convocation Hall can all be viewed via a self-guided tour or with a Law Society staff member during the summer months, starting at 1.15pm.

For a real treat, and if you've decided to go to the Momofuku Noodle Bar for

The handsome Campbell House Museum

dinner later, have lunch at the **Osgoode Hall Restaurant**, see ②, instead, which is located on the east side of the building, inside the elegant Convocation Hall. The menu is truly farm-to-table, featuring locally grown produce and meats. Note that there is a security check to enter the main building as it is still an active courthouse.

CAMPBELL HOUSE MUSEUM

Directly across from Osgoode Hall, on the west side of University Avenue, is the **Campbell House Museum** ⑤ (tel: 416-597-0227; www.camp-bellhousemuseum.ca; Tue–Fri 9.30am–4.30pm, Sat–Sun noon–4.30pm) dating from 1822. It was home to Upper Canada Chief Justice Sir William Campbell and his family until 1844, and continued to be the residence of prominent Torontonians until 1890, after which it was used for various companies as office space.

A fine example of Georgian architecture, the mansion's original location was actually 1.5km (1 mile) to the southeast of its current spot. It was moved here in 1972 to make way for a parking lot. Today it's a museum filled with period furniture and rotating art exhibits.

CANADA LIFE BUILDING

Next door, on the north side of Campbell House sits the grand, 15-floor

The pink sandstone Ontario Legislative Building

Beaux-Arts **Canada Life Building** 6. Constructed in 1931, it served as the headquarters for Canada Life, Canada's oldest, and at that time largest, insurance company. It still serves as office space today. The building is best known for its rooftop weather beacon whose color codes provide a four-times-daily local weather forecast. A steady green light equals clear conditions, steady red equals overcast, flashing red equals rain, and flashing white equals snow.

QUEEN'S PARK

After continuing northbound, passing further glass-clad and limestone structures housing consulates, medical institutes, and countless banks, this route ends at the beautiful **Queen's Park** 7, with the impressive **Ontario Legislative Building** 8 standing proudly within the center of the peaceful park. Built in the Romanesque Revival style, the building's main facade sports a neoclassical frieze featuring allegorical figures representing Art, Music, and Agriculture.

The oval, traditional British-designed Queen's Park officially opened in 1860, and is surrounded by campuses, including that of the University of Toronto. Significant statues and monuments, winding footpaths, and gorgeous rose gardens are featured throughout.

If time and remaining energy permits, the Royal Ontario Museum (see page 32) is just north of the park, as is the Gardiner Museum (see page 33) to the east and the fanciful Bata Shoe Museum (www.batashoemuseum.ca) – a must-visit for shoe fanatics – to the west.

Food and Drink

1 MOMOFUKU NOODLE BAR
190 University Avenue; tel: 647-253-6225; www.noodlebar-toronto.momofuku.com; daily L and D; $$
Multi-level, ultra modern, casual Asian eatery, with various noodle dishes including savory ramen on the menu, plus barbecued pork buns, crispy chicken wings, and plenty of vegetarian options, too. Their unusual desserts, such as the truffle cakes and crack pies, are quite delicious and worth leaving some room for.

2 OSGOODE HALL RESTAURANT
130 Queen Street West; tel: 416-947-3361; www.osgoodehallrestaurant.com; Mon–Fri L (Sept–June only); $$
Dine with lawyers taking a quick break from court here, under grand chandeliers and surrounded by stained-glass windows and row upon row of law books. Local farms supply most of the salad greens, fresh vegetables, and meats to complete the Canadiana menu. Try the Upper Canada Club sandwich, served since 1968, or order the value-priced daily three-course prix fixe menu.

The Art Gallery of Ontario, or AGO

CHINATOWN, KENSINGTON MARKET, AND LITTLE ITALY

See impressive fine art from all corners of the globe, then be temporarily transported to China, Italy, and sometime in the 1960s, picking up delightfully exotic snacks and trinkets along the way.

DISTANCE: 2.5km (1.6 miles) walking
TIME: Half day
START: Art Gallery of Ontario
END: Bar Raval
POINTS TO NOTE: The Art Gallery of Ontario (AGO) is closed on Mondays, so best avoid that day as the gallery is a must-see. And head out with an appetite, as there will be lots of tempting food options along this walk.

As one of Toronto's main attractions, the Art Gallery of Ontario is a major highlight on this tour, even if you only spend an hour inside (you could spend all day here with its 95,000-strong collection).

Buzzing with activity, Chinatown's streets are colorfully decorated with large signs, little curio shops, and lots of wonderful sidewalk stands overflowing with exotic fruits and vegetables. No less interesting is the counter-culture, and at times, gritty neighborhood of Kensington Market. To top off the busy day, a few moments or more in Little Italy are on the roster, with its fabulous eateries and bars.

ART GALLERY OF ONTARIO

From the St Patrick Station, walk west on Dundas Street. At McCaul Street, on the west corner the modern glass facade of the **Art Gallery of Ontario ❶** (tel: 416-979-6648; www.ago.ca; Tue–Sun 10.30am–5pm, Wed & Fri until 9pm; free Wed 6–9pm), designed by Toronto-native architect Frank Gehry stands out amongst the Victorian-era brick row houses and shops.

First opened in 1900 as the Art Museum of Toronto, it has since undergone four major renovations, the last as recently as 2018. The AGO is one of the largest galleries in North America and has an impressive collection of Canadian art as well as works from the Renaissance, African art, and Henry Moore pieces.

As part of the 2018 refurb, the former Centre for Canadian Art became the Centre for Indigenous and Canadian Art, reflecting the importance of

Café inside the AGO

presenting works by Canada's First Nations, Inuit, and Metis. In addition, the newly renovated space now includes a larger collection of works by Canadian female artists, such as Florence Carlyle and Joanne Tod. The layout of the Centre is set out in a thematic format, rather than in the usual chronological style; themes include historical connections from one artist to another, and environmental and political influences on the artists' work.

Henry Moore Sculpture Centre

Henry Moore (1898–1986) is perhaps best known for his semi-abstract monumental bronze sculptures, one of which was purchased by the City of Toronto in 1965 for the newly inaugurated Nathan Phillips Square (see page 31). Called *Three Way Piece No. 2*

or *The Archer*, this was a controversial purchase due to the cost and abstract nature of the sculpture. This purchase led Moore to donate a large collection of his work to the AGO between 1971 and 1974. Today it is the largest public collection of Moore's work in the world, comprising more than 900 bronze and plaster sculptures and works on paper, housed in the dedicated Henry Moore Sculpture Centre on the second floor.

Other highlights include the collections of the Canadian Group of Seven paintings (also on the second floor), works by the Dutch Masters, sketches by Michelangelo, large paintings by Willem de Kooning and Jackson Pollock, as well as iconic works by Frans Hals, Cézanne, Degas, Rothko, Matisse, Modigliani, Miró, Salvador Dalí, and Georgia O'Keeffe.

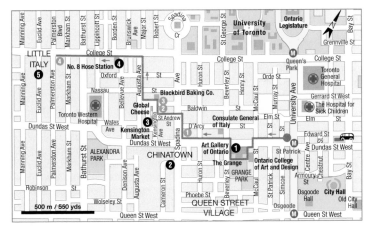

The striking table-top above the Sharpe Centre of Design

In addition to the vast galleries, the building also houses a library, artist-in-residence spaces, a research center, lecture hall, an excellent restaurant, café, coffee shop, and a gift shop. The AGO also frequently hosts events, including First Thursdays with live music, yoga tours, and stroller-friendly afternoon tours.

Farther south on McCaul Street, the checkerboard design of the **Sharpe Centre of Design – Ontario College of Art & Design** (tel: 416-977-6000; www.ocadu.ca; Wed noon–8pm, Thu–Fri noon–7pm, Sat–Sun noon–5pm; free), with its own little gallery, stands

Daily life in Chinatown

out, and just behind the AGO is **The Grange**. This historic brick house was built in 1817 as the first home of the AGO. It now contains some of the gallery's collections.

CHINATOWN

Back on Dundas Street, just past the AGO and on the north side of the street is the **Consulate General of Italy**, housed in the Chudleigh mansion, which was built in 1872. This is also the start of **Chinatown ②**, as can be seen by the colorful Chinese signs and stores lining Dundas Street.

Toronto has several Chinatowns, but this is the main one. Originally a Jewish community, it is sometimes referred to as Old Chinatown, and stretches along Spadina Avenue and Dundas Street West. And this Cantonese-speaking neighborhood isn't just home to residents with a Chinese heritage but also people from Thai, Vietnamese, Indian, and Japanese backgrounds, as is evident in the variety of Asian businesses and restaurants in the area.

Unusual herb and spice shops, sweet-smelling bakeries, little dim sum restaurants, and fresh produce stands overflowing with new foods to try fill the air with exotic scents. Walk toward Spadina Avenue and head north. For lunch, the cash-only, cheap and cheerful **Swatow Restaurant**, see ❶, is an authentic option. Pick from a range of noodle soups, rice dishes, and chow mein.

Bohemian Kensington Market

KENSINGTON MARKET

Across the street officially marks the border of **Kensington Market ❸**, with its Caribbean flavors, trendy boutiques, and friendly cafés. Crossing at St Andrew Street, walk west into the heart of this graffiti-clad, bohemian neighborhood, which is now a National Historic Site of Canada.

One of the city's best-known neighborhoods, Kensington Market is bordered by College Street in the north, Dundas Street West to the south, Spadina Avenue to the east, and Bathurst Street to the west. Eclectic to say the least, it is an edgy melting pot of cultures, dotted with colorful street art, and scented with wafts of spice, barbecue, and sweet pastries filling the narrow streets. Vintage stores spill their wares along the sidewalks where friendly, easy-going locals and wide-eyed visitors peruse the unusual goods on offer.

Kensington Market has always been home to a varied group of Torontonians, first as a Jewish community in the 1930s, then waves of Caribbean immigrants in the 1950s called the area their new home, followed by American political refugees in the 1970s during the Vietnam War. Today it's an amazing mix of European, Middle Eastern, Latin American, and Asian cultures, all blending together in, at times, a rather odd but wonderful fashion. Where else could you go for both Hungarian and Thai food under one roof? Yes, you can

Kensington gems

Blackbird Baking Co.
172 Baldwin Street; tel: 416-546-2280; www.blackbirdbakingco.com
A fantastic bakery that produces amazing sourdough breads, among other baked treats, both savory and sweet, including granola, lemon tarts, scones, and take-away sandwiches.

Cocktail Emporium
20 Kensington Avenue; tel: 416-858-2932; www.cocktailemporium.com
For the finest barware plus fun tiki decor and crucial cocktail ingredients, this bright shop is exactly what you need for anything drink and cocktail related.

Courage My Love
14 Kensington Avenue; tel: 416-979-1992
Possibly the best vintage shop around, with lovingly handpicked items spanning decades of retro styles from around the globe. Find cowboy boots, vintage purses, buttons and beads here also, plus housewares and other unique trinkets.

House of Spice
190 Augusta Avenue; tel: 416-593-9724; www.ehouseofspice.com
Selling herbs and spices from around the world since the early 1970s, this little family-owned shop can be sniffed out from miles away. Coffees, teas, hot sauces, and sea salts also make part of their exotic collection.

Popular Seven Lives, on Kensington Avenue

have that pork schnitzel with your pad thai noodles.

During the summer months, the whole area goes car-free on the last Sunday of the month (Pedestrian Sundays: from May until October), and visitors are treated to live and entertaining performances, farmers' markets with myriad food trucks, and plenty of great people-watching.

Turning north onto the narrow Kensington Avenue, Global Cheese is a must stop for picnic goodies. Or grab a quick bite from **Rasta Pasta**, see ❷, for

A sunny day in Kensington Market

Jamaican-fusion or **Seven Lives**, see ❸, for Mexican tacos, right next door.

Continue north to Baldwin Street and its cluster of varied eateries, head west onto Augusta Avenue, walking north to Oxford Street, passing by the Blue Banana Market, an excellent shop for unusual gifts and souvenirs ranging from kids clothing to Quebec-produced maple syrup.

No. 8 Fire Hose Station

Heading west onto Oxford Street, turn north onto Bellevue Avenue. At the corner of College Street and Bellevue, you'll see a modest, red-brick fire hall. Called **No. 8 Fire Hose Station** ❹, it was originally built in 1878, with a clock tower that was erected in 1899. The eight-story tower had a lookout at the top for the firefighters, and the hoses were hung to dry from here as well. In 1911, the fire hall received the first motorized fire truck in the city, replacing the horse-drawn fire wagons. It is one of the oldest, still-existing fire halls in the city.

Now you can either take the College Street streetcar westbound or walk a few more blocks west toward the lively Little Italy neighborhood, which officially starts at Bathurst Street and College Street.

LITTLE ITALY

Centered along College Street, between Bathurst Street and Ossington Avenue,

The Taste of Little Italy festival attracts the crowds

Toronto's **Little Italy** ❺ is certainly known for its inviting trattorias, lively pizzerias, and excellent espresso bars. Toronto's most delicious street festival is even celebrated here, called Taste of Little Italy, transforming the area into one huge street party every June.

However, this neighborhood is not as distinctly Italian as the name (and festival) might suggest. At least not so much as it used to be during its peak in the 1950s. Over the last five decades, people of Portuguese and Latin American heritage have set up shop and home in Little Italy also, bringing with them all the wonderful flavors and styles of their respective cultures in the form of bakeries, boutiques, and taco shops. During that time, another Italian enclave, called Corso Italia, just 4km (2.5 miles) north of Little Italy, along St Clair Avenue West, has grown and prospered and is now considered Toronto's second Little Italy.

Little Italy isn't just about pizzerias, cafés, and trattorias. It's also humming with some of the best bars in the city. Although not Italian, try the Spanish **Bar Raval**, see ❹, at College Street and Palmerston Boulevard, for excellent tapas and cocktails.

Food and Drink

❶ SWATOW RESTAURANT
309 Spadina Avenue; tel: 416-977-0601; www.swatowtoronto.com; daily L and D; $
Inexpensive and simple Chinese spot for fast, excellent and generous portions of noodle soup, fried rice dishes, and other comfort Cantonese foods. It's open late, but note that they accept cash only.

❷ RASTA PASTA
61 Kensington Avenue; tel: 647-501-4505; www.eatrastapasta.ca; Tue–Sun L; $
A Kensington Market staple, with long line-ups to prove it, this Jamaican take-out counter is famous for its jerk chicken. Try it in "The Vatican" – a grilled panini stuffed with the homemade, two-day marinated jerk chicken and fresh coleslaw.

❸ SEVEN LIVES
69 Kensington Avenue; tel: 416-393-4636; www.7lives.ca; daily L; $
Tiny and always busy Mexican take-out spot serving some of the best Californian and Baja-style tacos in the city. Note that this is a cash-only establishment.

❹ BAR RAVAL
505 College Street; tel: 647-344-8001; www.thisisbarraval.com; daily L and D; $$$
Sister restaurant to Bar Isabel, this fantastic casual Spanish tapas bar features a gorgeous Gaudí-inspired wooden interior. There's also a heated and covered patio space.

Kayaking between the Toronto Islands

THE TORONTO ISLANDS

Escape the busy city for the day and discover the tranquility of the Toronto Islands – considered the largest urban car-free community on the continent and only a short and pleasant ferry ride away from Downtown.

DISTANCE: 10km (6 miles) walking and ferry
TIME: Half day
START/END: Jack Layton Ferry Terminal
POINTS TO NOTE: Ferry tickets are for a return trip and can be purchased at the terminal or online (best option if you want to avoid the line). Ferries depart approximately every 15 minutes during the summer months. The total travel time for one way is about 13 minutes. There's also the option of chartering a boat, water taxi, or even taking a kayak or canoe across, though swimming is definitely not advised due to dangerous conditions. You can take bikes and strollers on the ferry, but during very busy summer season bikes may not be transported, so call ahead to check. While there are a few restaurants and snack bars on the islands, we recommend bringing a picnic lunch, perhaps picked out from the nearby St Lawrence Market.

Originally a sandbar peninsula, the Toronto Islands, which arch around the city's harbour, were cut adrift from the mainland by a violent storm in 1858. First used as a summer retreat by the Mississauga Nation, the islands went through various incarnations during the 20th century: they once hosted a baseball stadium, where slugger Babe Ruth hit his first professional home run, saw funfairs featuring horses diving from the pier, and even served as a training base for the Norwegian Air Force during World War II.

Today the tranquil islands make for a lovely day away from the hustle and bustle of the city, with secluded beaches, meandering bicycle trails, the village community, an amusement park, and memorable views as a bonus.

The three island areas – Centre, Ward's, and Hanlan's Point, plus various smaller islands comprise a total of approximately 242 hectares (600 acres) – and are all connected via a 5km (3-mile) network of pedestrian and bicycle-friendly paved paths, wooden boardwalks, and bridges.

A world away from the bustle of the city

The island community is a unique aspect of Toronto, with a group of residents intent on preserving their simple way of life. This is a place where visitors' cars are banned and many locals use wheelbarrows or golf buggies to move their wares.

Note that although the Billy Bishop Airport sits at the western end of the Toronto Islands, it is serviced by a different ferry system (and tunnel), at the foot of Bathurst Street. It is not accessible to visitors to the rest of the Toronto Islands.

Most restaurants and attractions are closed in winter, though the ferries oper-ate year-around. Cross-country skiing, snowshoeing, and ice-skating are just some of the activities happening during the wintertime on the islands.

JACK LAYTON FERRY TERMINAL

Starting at the foot of Bay Street at Queen's Quay, just east of the Westin Harbour Castle Hotel, three public ferries going on three separate routes take passengers across from the **Jack Layton Ferry Terminal** (tel: 416-392-8188; www.toronto.ca; daily departures in summer, limited services in winter) to Ward's Island, Centre Island,

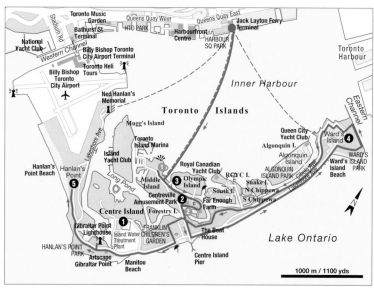

The pier on Centre Island

and Hanlan's Point. Since all the islands are connected, it doesn't really matter which ferry you take, though the most popular one is the ferry to the family-friendly Centre Island.

CENTRE ISLAND

After getting off the ferry, there's an information booth where you can pick up a map of the islands. **Centre Island** ❶ (tel: 416-392-8193; www.centreisland.ca), the largest island of all, has several dining options, or, if you packed a picnic, head to the large park areas or the sandy beach. There are a few playgrounds as well, splash and wading pools, a frisbee golf course, a maze,

The 'haunted' Gibraltar Point Lighthouse

landscaped gardens, beaches, plus shops to rent bicycles and boats. Small children will especially enjoy spending some time at the **Franklin Children's Garden**. Based on the *Franklin the Turtle* stories, it has storytelling and kids' gardening sessions, statues of book characters, a playhouse, and a 'snail trail' leading to a great viewpoint.

The **Toronto Island BBQ & Beer** restaurant, see ❶, immediately northwest of the ferry dock, boasts wonderful views from its large patio. You could have lunch there now or head back later for dinner.

Centreville Amusement Park

The highlight for families on Centre Island will probably be the **Centreville Amusement Park** ❷ (tel: 416-203-0405; www.centreisland.ca; May–Sept, hours vary), which is just northwest of the ferry docks. This is a vintage-style amusement park circa 19th century with a ferris wheel, carousel, miniature railway, swan ride, log flume, and a petting zoo. The park is free to wander around, but the rides require tickets. There are several snack bars for quick bites to eat, or try the casual **Carousel Café**, see ❷.

OLYMPIC ISLAND

Olympic Island ❸, accessed via a bridge just east of the ferry dock on Centre Island, has the best panoramic view of the Downtown skyline.

Fun times at the Centreville Amusement Park, Centre Island

WARD'S ISLAND

Heading south from the Centreville Amusement Park, across the bridge, head all the way east, passing between the cedar-hedge maze and **The Boat House** rental shop. This is now considered **Ward's Island ④**.

Actually a peninsula located at the eastern part of Centre Island, Ward's is a residential area with beautiful gardens and quiet streets lined with several-hundred colorful cottages dating back to the 1920s. The beaches north and on the easternmost tip are sandy and wonderful. Note that there are no restaurants or shops on the island. It does, however, have a flying disc (frisbee) golf course, several playgrounds, and a soccer field.

A 'HAUNTED' LIGHTHOUSE

Following the paths west and backtracking a bit toward the southwestern and west end of the island, you will pass by the haunted **Gibraltar Point Lighthouse** (closed to the public).

Begun in 1808, it is one of Toronto's oldest buildings. According to local lore, the lighthouse is haunted by its first keeper John Paul Radelmüller, who was murdered here in 1815 by a group of soldiers from Fort York searching for his bootlegged beer. But they had too much to drink and a dispute broke out, culminating in the keeper's murder. The inebriated soldiers, so it is claimed, tried to conceal their crime by chopping apart the corpse and hiding the remains.

HANLAN'S POINT

Further along, you'll reach **Hanlan's Point ⑤**. Hanlan's is best known for its clothing-optional beach – **Hanlan's Point Beach**, further up Lakeshore Avenue then turning onto Beach Road. Note that since Lake Ontario is generally considered too polluted for swimming, most visitors stick to sunbathing.

Food and Drink

① TORONTO ISLAND BBQ & BEER
Centre Island; tel: 416-234-2345; www.centreisland.ca; Mon–Fri 11.30am–8pm, Sat–Sun 11.30am–9.30pm, June–Sept; $$
Casual waterside eatery with some of best views of Toronto's skyline, especially from the huge patio. Specialties include smoked meats, poutine, burgers, and sandwiches, plus there's a kids menu and, of course, plenty of beer on tap.

② CAROUSEL CAFÉ
Centre Island; tel: 416-203-0405; www.centreisland.ca; daily 11am–5pm, Apr–Oct; $$
Relaxed café in the Centreville Amusement Park serving pub fare such as burgers, sandwiches, pastas, and fish & chips. There is also a kids menu and an outdoor patio.

Costumed guides give the low-down on colonial life at Fort York

FORT YORK
AND WEST QUEEN WEST

History buffs will thoroughly appreciate this walking tour,
and for music and art lovers, it has a perfect ending.

DISTANCE: 6km (3.7 miles) walking and streetcar
TIME: Half day
START: Fort York National Historic Site
END: Bang Bang Ice Cream & Bakery
POINTS TO NOTE: Families with kids of all ages will appreciate this route as it includes plenty of outdoor time in wide open spaces, which also means that it is best done in fair weather.

Toronto is fortunate to have a well-preserved public site, that is essentially the city's birthplace. This tour takes you there followed by a meal and drink in one of the city's best-loved neighborhoods.

FORT YORK NATIONAL HISTORIC SITE

From Union Station, take the 509 Harbourfront streetcar westbound toward the CNE Exhibition grounds, getting off at Fleet Street and Fort York Boulevard. Walk north to the **Fort York National Historic Site ❶** (tel: 416-392-6907; www.fortyork.ca; daily 10am–5pm).

Built by British Army General and Lieutenant Governor John Graves Simcoe in 1793 to defend the new capital of Upper Canada, known then as York, this 17.4-hectare (43-acre) site is considered Toronto's birthplace. In 1813, Fort York was invaded and almost entirely destroyed by the US Army and Navy during the War of 1812, but it was quickly rebuilt and in continuous use by the British and Canadian military until 1880. It was subsequently used as a military training site during both world wars.

The buildings here are among the oldest in the city and include barracks, powder magazines, and officer's quarters featuring artillery and costumes. There is also an audiovisual presentation of the birth of Toronto: Fort York and the Birth of Urban Toronto. During the summer months, the Fort York Guard do presentations in period costumes, and workshops and festivals are also hosted here. You can also stroll through the Fort's Community Garden.

Exit south, walking from the main visitor center onto Fort York Boulevard and south to Lake Shore Boulevard West. You can stroll through the **Corona-**

Cinesphere

tion Park along the way. Continue on, past Inukshuk Park, until you reach the Ontario Place West Entrance. Now head south along the pedestrianised bridges and pods to reach the Cinesphere.

CINESPHERE

Located in Ontario Place, a public park made up of three artificial islands, **Cinesphere ②** (tel: 416-314-9938; www. ontarioplace.com; daily, showtimes vary; charge for movies) was the world's first permanent IMAX movie theatre (1971). Watching a movie inside the 35m (115ft) wide triodetic dome is truly exciting.

From the Cinesphere, walk back up to Lake Shore Boulevard West, crossing north to Exhibition Place.

EXHIBITION PLACE

Exhibition Place ③ includes various parks, sports facilities, such as the BMO Field (see page 71), and convention centers. Each year, from mid-August to early September, the Canadian National Exhibition (CNE) (tel: 416-263-3330; www.theex. com) is held on these grounds, with exhibits on agriculture, food, arts and crafts, plus a fun fair, live music, and plenty of food trucks.

THE DRAKE HOTEL

From Dufferin Street you can take the 29 Bus northbound to Queen Street West, then walk east a few blocks to **The Drake Hotel ④** (see page 89).

Housed in a 19th-century brick building that's been a hotel since 1890, The Drake is one of the city's best-known music

Simpler times at the Black Creek Pioneer village

venues, with nightly performances in the subterranean **Drake Underground** (see page 103) space. For lunch at **The Drake Hotel**, see ❶, choose from the art-filled ground-level restaurant lounge and bar area, the casual café, or the sunny rooftop patio.

OSSINGTON AVENUE

Afterward, continue to stroll west along Queen Street West, where you can shop for hip clothing, shoes, and gifts if you wish. Head north onto Ossington Avenue and have dinner at **Union**, see ❷. Have another dessert at **Bang Bang Ice Cream & Bakery**, see ❸ and then walk back to The Drake Hotel or to another bar, such as **The Dakota Tavern** (see page 103) or the **Bellwoods Brewery** (see page 102) for live music and a nightcap.

Black Creek Pioneer Village

For more early city history, make your way to the Black Creek Pioneer Village in North York, about an hour on the bus. This open-air heritage museum recreates 19th-century local life with over 40 heritage buildings containing period furnishings, while costumed staffers entertain with re-enactments and craft making. (1000 Murray Ross Parkway, North York; tel: 416-726-1733; www.blackcreek.ca; Mon–Fri 10am–5pm, Sat–Sun 11am–5pm, Apr–Dec).

Food and Drink

❶ THE DRAKE HOTEL

1150 Queen Street West; tel: 416-531-5042; www.thedrake.ca; daily B, L, and D; $$

Pick your spot to eat, whether it's the lounge, café, or rooftop patio, and go for a freshly squeezed juice and the Drake Burger with an addition of truffle butter. Finish off with a decadent dessert such as the tarte au chocolat, consisting mostly of rich chocolate mousse.

❷ UNION

72 Ossington Avenue; tel: 416-850-0093; www.union72.ca; daily L and D; $$$

Inspired by the classic Parisian bistros, Union is an intimate spot for fine dining in a relaxed and comfortable atmosphere. Try the elk sliders served on soft challah bread, the smoked and braised sticky ribs, and for dessert, the crème brûlée.

❸ BANG BANG ICE CREAM & BAKERY

93a Ossington Avenue; tel: 647-348-1900; no website; Tue–Thu 3–10pm, Fri–Sun 1–10pm; $

Ossington Strip favorite, known for their custom-made ice cream sandwiches created with house-made ice cream and cookies. The flavors of ice cream come in traditional classics with a twist, such as burnt toffee or pink lemonade, and really exotic ones such as lychee and rosewater or peanut butter and grape jelly.

The extravagant Casa Loma

NORTH OF THE CITY

Visit Toronto's mock castle, go inside a Victorian-era home, and peek around a toll-keeper's cottage from the 1830s. Then continue on, exploring Koreatown, with its authentic eateries, gift shops, and karaoke bars.

DISTANCE: 3km (1.9 miles) walking or partly by bus.
TIME: Half day
START: Casa Loma
END: Korean Village Restaurant
POINTS TO NOTE: The Tollkeeper's Cottage on this tour is only open on Saturdays and the Spadina Museum is by guided tour only, though these tours are quite frequent during the summer months. Getting to Casa Loma, say from Union Station, is simple. Just take the line 1 northbound (Vaughan Metropolitan Centre direction) and step out at Dupont Station, then proceed to walk north along Spadina Road for about 10 minutes and you'll reach the castle.

Toronto is full of historic architecture, from the old barracks at Fort York (see page 60), to the sturdy brick warehouses at the Distillery Historic District (see page 43), and all the pretty Victorian homes scattered around the city's neighborhoods. None compete with the grandeur of Casa Loma however, and the Spadina Museum next door is filled with furnishings that would have been inside the mansion. To keep things humble, a look inside a toll-keeper's cottage ends the tour before grabbing a bite to eat in Koreatown.

CASA LOMA

Surprisingly grand and elegant, **Casa Loma ❶** (tel: 416-923-1171; www.casa-loma.ca; daily 9.30am–5pm) was built in 1911 for Sir Henry Pellatt, a wealthy financier who was responsible for bringing hydro-electricity to the city. At the time of construction, Casa Loma was the biggest private residence ever built in Canada. In Gothic Revival style, the mansion took nearly 300 workers over three years to complete.

On five lush acres of beautifully groomed gardens, Casa Loma has 98 rooms and originally had unusual features for a home at that time, including a central vacuum system, a bidet, an elevator, and several bowling alleys – the latter never having been completed as Pellatt ran out of funds.

Lady Pellatt's suite, painted in Wedgwood Blue

Visitors can explore the lavishly decorated rooms with some authentic period furnishings, discover secret storage areas and passageways, or take in panoramic views over Toronto from one of the towers.

Casa Loma also offers an exciting and entertaining Escape Series – theatrical escape games with live actors, offering a unique and immersive game experience. Check the Casa Loma website for the current event schedule.

SPADINA MUSEUM

Right next door to Casa Loma is the city's **Spadina Museum ❷** (tel: 416-392-6910; www.toronto.ca; by guided tours only, hours vary), offering a glimpse of domestic life in Toronto through the lens of the Austin family from 1900 to 1930. The site includes six structures, one of which is the main three-story house built in 1866 with original furnishings. The interior of the house and outbuildings can be seen by guided tour only, though the Victorian-Edwardian gardens are open to the public and visitors are free to wander there.

The property was originally purchased in 1866 by businessman and financier James Austin, originally from Northern Ireland and founder of the Dominion Bank, known today as the Toronto-Dominion Bank. At first Austin and his family farmed the land, and later subdivided it and sold the majority of it, keeping just under 6 acres that included an orchard, grape arbor and a kitchen garden, along with the English-style formal lawns.

The historic main house illustrates the change of art, decor, technologies, and architecture from the 1860s through the 1930s, including Victorian, Edwardian, Arts and Crafts, Art Deco, and Colonial Revival styles.

TOLLKEEPER'S COTTAGE

From the Spadina Museum, walk west down Austin Terrace, veering south. Austin Terrace becomes Walmer Road. Then turn west along Davenport Road to Bathurst Street. The northwest corner of the intersection is home to the

Korean bibimbap

Welcome to Koreatown

Tollkeeper's Cottage ❸ (tel: 416-515-7546; www.tollkeeperscottage.ca; Sat 11am–5pm; by donation) – one of the oldest homes in the city, built in 1835. It's now a small museum with sparse period furnishings reflecting the simpler times of the toll collector.

For lunch, walk south down Bathurst Street, turning east onto Dupont Street, to the corner of Dupont and Howland Avenue where **Schmaltz Appetizing**, see ❶, offers a choice of Jewish deli items. You are now on the border of **The Annex**, a hip studenty neighborhood.

KOREATOWN

From Bathurst Street and Dupont Street, catch the number 7 bus southbound or walk for about 1.5km (1 mile) south to Bloor Street West. You're now in **Koreatown** ❹ – a vibrant little neighborhood full of inexpensive eateries, karaoke bars, and novelty gift shops, ending at the large Christie Pits Park.

Toronto has about 50,000 people living in the city that identify themselves as having a Korean heritage, many of whom have opened up businesses around Koreatown – a small stretch along Bloor Street, between Christie and Bathurst Streets. Restaurants and bakeries serving authentic Korean fare, novelty gift shops with imported Korean goods, and grocery stores carrying specialty Korean products can all be found in Koreatown. Most of the city's karaoke bars have settled here (karaoke may be a Japanese

invention, but it's also hugely popular in South Korea). To experience the full flavor of this fun neighborhood, the annual Korean Dano Spring Festival in June, with its martial arts demonstrations and traditional music, is a great opportunity to enjoy more of Korea's culture, right here in Toronto.

End the day with an authentic Korean meal at the **Korean Village Restaurant**, see ❷, and if you're still full of energy, head out to **Coda** (see page 106) – one of the city's hottest nightclubs.

Food and Drink

❶ SCHMALTZ APPETIZING

414 Dupont Street; tel: 647-350-4261; www.schmaltzappetizing.com; daily B and L; $

Jewish deli in The Annex neighborhood with fantastic, easy-on-the-budget bagel sandwiches filled with whipped cream cheese, freshly sliced lox, capers, and onions. Eat inside or enjoy it out on their little patio.

❷ KOREAN VILLAGE RESTAURANT

628 Bloor Street West; tel: 416-536-0290; www.koreanvillagetoronto.com; daily L and D; $$

A staple of Koreatown, this homey, family-run authentic Korean restaurant has a choice of private rooms and booth seating. Ask for the table BBQ for a traditional and fun way to cook your own food.

Jellyfish ballet at Ripley's Aquarium of Canada

ALONG THE PATH

Chances are that your visit to Toronto may include a rainy day or two.
Or perhaps it's a heatwave during the summertime and the temperatures
are scorchingly high. Even on a nice day, visiting an aquarium and a lush
conservatory can be wonderful, and you may even lose some of the crowds.

DISTANCE: 7km (4.3 miles) some walking, but mostly subway and streetcar
TIME: Half day
START: Ripley's Aquarium of Canada
END: Pai Northern Thai Kitchen
POINTS TO NOTE: On a wet or cold day, the PATH network of tunnels is convenient and connects various attractions around the city.

PATH is a network of more than 30km (19 miles) of underground pedestrian tunnels and elevated walkways, connecting attractions, shopping malls, office towers, hotels, and subway stations. The CN Tower, Ripley's Aquarium of Canada, Scotiabank Arena, and Rogers Centre are all connected via PATH, specifically, via an enclosed and elevated walkway called the SkyWalk, which connects to Union Station. The Hockey Hall of Fame, Roy Thomson Hall, City Hall, and the CF Toronto Eaton Centre are also connected via PATH. See the city of Toronto website, www. toronto.ca, for a complete map of the network.

On this particular tour you'll visit the famous aquarium, plus a lovely indoor garden site, and a spicy lunch or dinner at the end to further ward off cool temperatures.

RIPLEY'S AQUARIUM OF CANADA

Begin this route at **Ripley's Aquarium of Canada ❶** (tel: 647-351-3474; www.ripleyaquariums.com; daily 9am–11pm, with occasional earlier closures for events), where you can get a close look at sharks, stingrays, turtles, and 450 other marine and freshwater species. Little ones will love the touch exhibits, and the daily dive shows are exciting for the whole family.

The shark tunnel is of course the big draw here and there is an exciting opportunity to 'sleep with sharks'. Indeed, for a slumber party to remember, groups of children can stay overnight in the Dangerous Lagoon shark tunnel (8pm–9am). Another highlight, the Planet Jellies, one of the largest jel-

Cheers at the Steam Whistle Brewery

lyfish tanks in the world, will mesmerize you with its color-changing displays.

The **CN Tower** (see page 37) is right next door to the aquarium if you haven't visited it yet. If you're feeling thirsty, visit the award-winning **Steam Whistle Brewery**, see ❶, just south across the road from the aquarium and tower. Go on an informative and fun tour of the brewery, which is housed in a historic brick railroad roundhouse, and taste a few of their refreshing beers.

TD CENTRE

From the aquarium, follow the PATH east to Union Station then north, passing the Royal Bank Plaza, all the way to the TD South Tower, one of six glass and steel towers collectively called the **TD Centre** ❷. Built between 1967–91, it boasted German-American architect Ludwig Mies van der Rohe as one of its original design consultants. His style permeates trough the dark color palette, the use of steel, granite, marble, wood, and glass, and the strict ordered aesthetic of each modern structure.

Toronto Dominion Gallery of Inuit Art

Inside the TD South Tower, beginning on the ground level and up a flight of stairs to the mezzanine, is the **Toronto Dominion Gallery of Inuit Art** ❸ (tel: 416-982-8473; www.td.com; Mon–Fri 8am–6pm, Sat–Sun 10am–4pm; free). On display here are some 200 original soap-

The old Toronto Stock Exchange building

stone, bone, antler, and ivory sculptures, in addition to prints and ceramics, all the work of Inuit artists from Canada's arctic, mostly dating from the 1940s–60s. The collection was founded in 1967 by the Toronto Dominion Bank to commemorate Canada's 100th birthday, a celebration of both the country's past and future via art. The actual gallery didn't open to the public until 1982.

TORONTO STOCK EXCHANGE AND DESIGN EXCHANGE

Just northeast from the TD South Tower, still along the PATH, you'll come across the historic old **Toronto Stock Exchange** ❹. Built in 1937, the Art Deco limestone facade features a carved frieze

Forno Cultura fare

designed by Canadian painter Charles Comfort depicting the various industries whose stocks traded inside. Comfort also painted the four large murals overlooking the old exchange floor. The stock exchange relocated to its current headquarters at King and York Streets in 1983 and the building now hosts the **Design Exchange** ❺ (tel: 416-363-6121; www. dx.org; Wed–Fri 9am–5pm, Sat–Sun noon–4.30pm; free), a small museum dedicated to Canadian design from the last six decades, from furniture design to house appliances, clothing, and graphics.

FIRST CANADIAN PLACE

Across the street from the TD Centre towers stands **First Canadian Place** ❻, Canada's tallest skyscraper at 298 meters (978ft). Built in 1975, it houses the headquarters of the Bank of Montreal, three floors of shops, a food court, and various services such as a medical center, spa, and post office. Stop by **Forno Cultura**, see ❷, on the Concourse Level, for a light bite to eat: Italian sandwiches, salads, sweet pastries, and beautifully strong coffee.

ALLAN GARDENS CONSERVATORY

Follow the PATH down to Union Station, then head north on subway line 1 (Vaughan Metropolitan Centre direction) and get out at the Museum station. You're now at the **Royal Ontario Museum** (see page 32), and you could pop in here if

Allan Gardens Conservatory   *Cacti at the Arid House*

you wish. Or get out at Queen's Station, then board the 506 Carlton streetcar eastbound, getting out at Carlton Street and Sherbourne Street where the **Allan Gardens Conservatory** ⑦ (tel: 416-392-7288; www.toronto.ca; daily 10am–5pm; free) surrounds you in tropical warmth and exotic plant life.

Built in 1858, Allan Gardens is one of the oldest parks in Toronto. The conservatory here comprises of two tropical houses dedicated to orchids and bromeliads, while cooler (but still balmy) temperate houses are home to camellias, jasmine, citrus trees, and other exotics, in addition to a little waterfall feature and a pond filled with koi fish. The lush

Palm House is filled with banana trees, bamboo, tropical vines, and palm trees, naturally, while the Arid House has cacti and succulents. There's a playground on site, and even an off-leash area for four-legged friends, though these latter two are outside and uncovered.

Now it's time for dinner, or perhaps it's still lunchtime. Either way, take the 506 Carlton streetcar westbound, getting off at the College Station. Take the line 1 subway southbound to the St Andrew Station and walk west along King Street West for two blocks, turn north onto Duncan Street, one block, and have dinner at **Pai Northern Thai Kitchen**, see ❸ – the city's top Thai restaurant.

Food and Drink

① STEAM WHISTLE BREWERY
255 Bremner Boulevard; tel: 416-362-2337; www.steamwhistle.ca; Mon–Sat 11am–6pm, Sun 11am–5pm; $
It's a brewery, not a brewpub, so food isn't offered here, except for some bar snacks. What you come here for is the terrific beer. You can sit at the bar and order what you wish or go on a tour. Tours are daily and start at 11.30am until about 5pm, and run every 30 minutes. There is a charge for the tour.

② FORNO CULTURA
First Canadian Place, 100 King Street West; tel: 416-504-8305; www.fornocultura.com; Mon–Fri 7.30am–6pm; $

An artisanal Italian bakery supplying Torontonians with the most amazing paninis, cakes, and biscotti. Try the perfectly thin-sliced prosciutto panini on sourdough. The meats and cheeses used in their devious goods are locally sourced. Pick up freshly baked breads here, too, made with organic flour.

③ PAI NORTHERN THAI KITCHEN
18 Duncan Street; tel: 416-901-4724; www. paitoronto.com; Mon–Sat L and D, Sun D; $$
Thai Chef Nuit shares her amazing family recipes, street market dishes, and other creative offerings at this top Thai restaurant. The atmosphere is lively here, and reservations are recommended, even if there's ample seating – it's busy here every single night.

HOME OF THE TORONTO ⌾ BLUE JAYS

The Rogers Centre, home of the Blue Jays

ALL THINGS SPORTS

Even if you're not normally a big sports fan, experiencing the thrill of watching a live hockey, baseball, basketball, soccer, or football game is highly memorable and lots of fun.

> **DISTANCE:** 4km (2.5 miles) walking, streetcar, not all done in one day
> **TIME:** Half day
> **START:** Scotiabank Arena
> **END:** Hockey Hall of Fame
> **POINTS TO NOTE:** From Union Station it's just a few minutes' walk south to the Scotiabank Arena and southwest to the Rogers Centre. The BMO Field is farther west and is reached via the 509 Harbourfront streetcar westbound. The Hockey Hall of Fame is a five-minute walk east from Union Station, along Front Street West.

Torontonians are sports mad, and dropping in on a hockey game can give visitors an unforgettable insight on the city and its people. While this tour doesn't expect you to be able to go to a hockey, baseball, basketball, soccer, or a football game all in one day, it will cover all five options. Even watching a game on a big TV screen in a sports bar or seeing the Stanley Cup up close at the Hockey Hall of Fame can be a hoot.

SCOTIABANK ARENA

If you are visiting Toronto between the months of October to April, you may be able to get your hands on some tickets to watch a live NHL Toronto Maple Leafs hockey game at the **Scotiabank Arena ❶** (tel: 1-855-465-3237 ticketmaster for

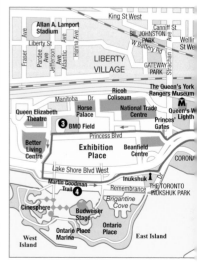

A match at BMO Field

Toronto Maple Leafs, 1-855-727-8677 for Toronto Raptors; www.scotiabankarena.com). Conversely, you can get tickets to watch the NBA Toronto Raptors basketball team (and maybe catch a glimpse of their ambassador, local rap star, Drake). Otherwise, the area outside of the Scotiabank Arena, called Maple Leaf Square, shows the live games on a giant, 15x24-meter (50x80ft) outdoor TV screen.

ROGERS CENTRE

The **Rogers Centre** ❷ (tel: 416-341-1234 box office; www.rogerscentre.com) west of the Scotiabank Arena, hosts baseball games from April through October of the local Toronto Blue Jays

MLB team. With its fully retractable roof, this stadium is ideal for most weather conditions. Other events take place at the stadium as well, including wrestling, cricket, and major concerts. Tours of the stadium are available and can take you through a museum, the Blue Jays Hall of Fame, a press box, and a luxury suite.

BMO FIELD

Farther west is the outdoor **BMO Field** ❸ (tel: 1-855-985-4625 ticketmaster for Toronto FC, 1-855-462-7467 ticketmaster for Toronto Argonauts; www.bmofield.com), located at the Exhibition Place, and is home to the Toronto FC Major League Soccer team and the Toronto Argonauts

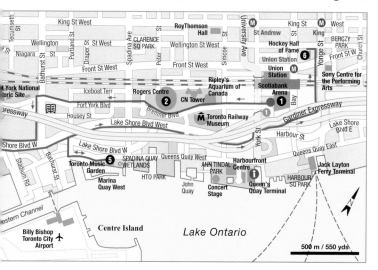

Humber Bay Arch Bridge, along the Martin Goodman Trail

of the Canadian Football League (CFL). The Toronto FC games are from March to October, while the Toronto Argonauts play from June to November.

MARTIN GOODMAN TRAIL

For a leisurely walk, fitful run, or a scenic bike ride, the **Martin Goodman Trail ❹**, is a 56km (35 mile) multi-use path that extends all along Toronto's waterfront, from one end of the city to the other. It is part of the much longer Great Lakes Waterfront Trail, which is over 3,000km (1,865 miles) long and connects 140 communities along the shores of the Great Lakes region.

TORONTO MUSIC GARDEN

If you only fancy a short walk on the Martin Goodman Trail, start the trail south of the Scotiabank Arena, accessing it via Bay Street down by the Westin Harbour Castle hotel. Follow it west, passing by the Harbourfront Centre (see page 34), and stopping at the **Toronto Music Garden ❺** (tel: 416-973-4000; www.toronto.ca; open dawn till dusk; free, charge for self-guided audio players). This waterfront park was created by renowned cellist Yo-Yo Ma and landscape designer Julie Moir Messervy. Inspired by Bach's Suite No.1 in G Major for unaccompanied cello, the park has winding paths flanked by manicured flower beds and large boulders. There's often free live, classical music performances here in the summer afternoons.

SPORTS BAR

Lots of sports bars and pubs will show any significant games on big screens. For a pre-game or post-game bite to eat and drink, the **Real Sports Bar & Grill**, see ❶, is a perfect choice. Plus it's located right next to the Scotiabank Arena on Maple Leaf Square.

HOCKEY HALL OF FAME

A mecca for sports fans, and fun for anyone with its interactive multimedia exhibits, games, and famous hockey memorabilia, the **Hockey Hall of Fame ❻** (see page 39) is the place for hockey aficionados. The main draw here is seeing the Stanley Cup trophy – hockey's holy grail.

Food and Drink

❶ REAL SPORTS BAR & GRILL

15 York Street; tel: 416-815-7325; www. realsports.ca; daily 11am–midnight, until 2am Thu–Sat; $$

Claimed to be Canada's largest sports bar, located right at the heart of the action on Maple Leaf Square, any sports fan will be at home here with a 12-meter (39ft) HD TV screen, nearly 200 smaller screens, over 100 beers on tap, and a pretty good pub menu as well.

Cheetah love at the Toronto Zoo

TORONTO ZOO AND OTHER FAMILY-FRIENDLY EXCURSIONS

Most of Toronto's attractions and restaurants cater for young children as well as for older children and adults. However, this tour will head out of the city a bit farther to explore a family favorite, the Toronto Zoo.

DISTANCE: 64km (40 miles) driving or subway and bus
TIME: Full day
START/END: Toronto Zoo
POINTS TO NOTE: The Toronto Zoo is a two-hour ride northeast with public transportation, starting from Union Station on line 1 (Finch direction) to Bloor-Yonge Station, then on line 2 east to Kennedy Station, and then the 86A bus directly to the zoo. Driving by car will take about 30 minutes.

Depending on how far you feel like traveling with children, there are options of family-friendly attractions throughout the Downtown area and farther out. A day trip to the Toronto Islands (see page 56) makes for a wonderful, family-friendly outing, provided the weather is cooperating. Back on the mainland, the CN Tower (see page 37) offers a thrilling elevator ride to the top, with views that will blow kids' minds. Down on the ground again, Ripley's Aquarium of Canada (see page 66) is perfect on a rainy day, while an afternoon at the Royal Ontario Museum (see page 32) with its dinosaur displays and eerie bat cave will satisfy little naturalists.

For mini sports enthusiasts, the Hockey Hall of Fame (see page 39), with its competitive games and hockey treasures, will provide at least an hour or two or fun. Head inside the nearby St Lawrence Market (see page 39) for snack and lunch options that won't leave even the pickiest eaters hungry. Casa Loma (see page 63) can be interesting to older children who'll appreciate the secret passageways, towers, and antique stables. Even Fort York (see page 60), with its costumed staff and re-enactments, can easily fill up and hour or two.

For an out of town attraction, the Toronto Zoo is well worth the drive. A whole day can be easily spent here, with not only animals to see but also rides to go on, a splash zone to play in, and an interesting Wildlife Health Centre to visit where visitors can catch a behind-the-scenes glimpse of the work done there.

The zoo starts here

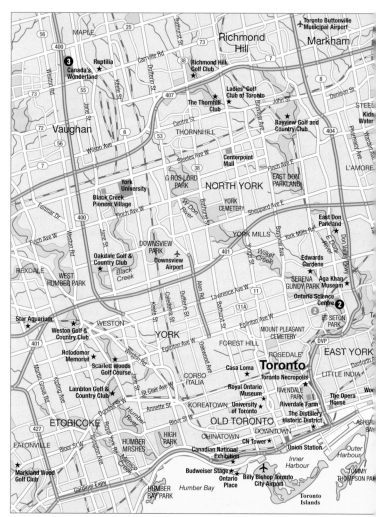

Flamboyant peacock   *Pandas are always a hit*

TORONTO ZOO

The **Toronto Zoo** ❶ (tel: 416-392-5929; www.torontozoo.com; daily 9am–7pm, earlier closures in winter) is the largest zoo in Canada, and one of the largest in North America at 710 acres (287 hectares), featuring a varied terrain, from dense forest, to valleys, rivers, and savanna.

The zoo, which is modeled partly on the famous San Diego Zoo, is divided into seven zoogeographic regions, with over 5,000 animals representing over 450 species housed in tropical pavilions and natural outdoor environments. All the exciting species are here, including apes, tigers, leopards, lions, rhinos, hippos, meerkats, komodo dragons, camels, pandas, polar bears, and raptors, plus a selection of Canadian wildlife. The zoo also has an extensive breeding, recovery, and reintroduction program.

Six miles (10km) of walking trails crisscross the zoo, or you can hop on the Zoomobile, an open train that zips around, if walking becomes too much. Strollers and wagons are available for rent as well. Lots of snack bars and restaurants are onsite and the zoo allows you to bring in your own food as well, with picnic tables set out at various locations. **Smoke's Poutinerie**, see ❶, has two locations in the zoo, one in the Front Courtyard just north of the main entrance, and one just outside of the African Savanna region.

Exhibit at the Ontario Science Centre

ONTARIO SCIENCE CENTRE

The **Ontario Science Centre** ❷ (tel: 416-696-1000; www.ontario-sciencecentre.ca; daily 10am–5pm, Sat until 8pm) is a splendid science museum located about 11km (7 miles) northeast of downtown Toronto, with over 800 interactive, high-tech exhibits that the whole family can enjoy. High-

lights include a rainforest complete with poison dart frogs, a touchable tornado, a cave, and a coral reef, as well as meteorites from Mars. There's also an indoor rock-climbing wall and an IMAX theater that shows nature films on a giant dome screen.

For dining options, the Science Centre has three cafés and two restaurants on site, offering the standard fare of such snacks as pastries, sandwiches, salads, burgers, hot dogs, and pizza. If you've driven out here, try heading west, about 2.4km (1.5 miles), to **Adamson Barbecue**, see ❷, open for lunch only.

Getting up close at the Ontario Science Centre

Free family fun

Riverdale Farm (tel: 416-392-6794; www.riverdalefarmtoronto.ca; daily 9am–5pm; free)
Located in the Cabbagetown neighborhood, northeast of downtown Toronto, is the Riverdale Farm. This is a 3-hectare (7.4-acre) working farm, originally at the site of a zoo that began in 1888. The farm is free and open to the public year-round, and features chickens, goats, pigs, sheep, cows, horses, donkeys, and more, some of which can be petted and fed.

High Park (tel: 416-338-0338; www.toronto.ca; llama pens Sat–Sun 11.30am–2pm)
This lakefront, 161-hectare (400-acre) park west of Toronto's downtown core has a free zoo with llamas, which you can feed and pet, and various other friendly animals. The park also has several playgrounds, snack bars, ponds, lots of trails, a museum, an outdoor pool, and a nature center.

Canada's Wonderland, a fun day out

Feast on succulent brisket, spare ribs, pulled pork, sausages, and all the sides you can dream of.

CANADA'S WONDERLAND

A must for thrill-seekers, **Canada's Wonderland** ❸ (tel: 905-832-8131; www.canadaswonderland.com; daily 10am–10pm June–Sept) is a huge amusement park an hour's drive north of Toronto. As well as your favorite cartoon characters wandering around, it features over 60 rides, a water park, miniature golf, an arcade, and plenty more.

The park is divided up into nine zones, with three zones dedicated to younger visitors, but the wild rollercoasters are found throughout. The Yukon Striker, new in 2019, will be the world's fastest, tallest, and longest dive coaster – the type with a near-vertical drop that's definitely not for the faint-hearted!

A patriotic display at High Park

The park has tons of cafés, snack shacks, and eateries to keep you full and satisfied all day long. And if you are here all day, you may want to consider purchasing an All Day Dining Plan that allows you to eat a meal at each of the participating restaurants for one relatively low price.

Food and Drink

❶ SMOKE'S POUTINERIE

Toronto Zoo; tel: 416-392-5929; www.smokespoutinerie.com; daily B, L, D; $

A Toronto original, this poutinerie chain is fast becoming a global hit, for fries covered in gravy and cheese curds, that is. Try the Double Pork poutine with chipotle pulled pork and double-smoked bacon. No need for seconds after this satisfying dish.

❷ ADAMSON BARBECUE

176 Wicksteed Avenue; tel: 416-316-5216; www.adamsonbarbecue.com; L Tue–Sat; $$

Central Texas-style barbecue, serving home-made brisket, spare ribs, turkey, pulled pork, sausages, and traditional sides such as potato salad, cornbread, and coleslaw. Order as a plate, a sandwich, or if you're with a few people, as a platter. Desserts are home-made as well; be tempted by the coconut cream pie. Afterwards, you'll need to roll yourself to the car.

NIAGARA FALLS
AND THE WINE COUNTRY

Niagara Falls is just a 1.5-hour drive from downtown Toronto. You can choose to go just for the day, or spend a night in the area, exploring the famous wine-making region and charming towns for a few days.

DISTANCE: 300km (186 miles) return trip driving or public transportation from downtown Toronto, 50km (31 miles) driving within Niagara Falls and surrounding area.

TIME: Full day to two days

START/END: Niagara Falls

POINTS TO NOTE: It takes about 1.5 hours to drive from downtown Toronto to Niagara Falls, following the QEW (Queen Elizabeth Way) highway. Public transportation (buses) connects Toronto to Burlington and then to Niagara Falls daily, and it takes about 2.5 hours. GO Train, part of the GTA public transit system, has a seasonal train service taking passengers from Union Station to Niagara Falls Train Station. VIA Rail, Canada's national passenger rail service, also offers an all-year-round service from Toronto to Niagara Falls. Both have daily services, sometimes twice a day with VIA Rail, and travel time is about 2 hours one way. Niagara Falls Train Station is 4km (2.5 miles) from the actual falls so you need to take a bus or taxi from there.

Depending on whether you have your own transportation, public transportation, or if you're heading to the magnificent and mighty Niagara Falls on a tour, you may want to consider exploring the area just outside of the town of Niagara Falls while you're out there. Some tour companies will incorporate a side trip to a winery or two as well.

NIAGARA FALLS

Created by the Wisconsin glaciation about 10,000 years ago, **Niagara Falls ❶** (www. niagaraparks.com), which can always be viewed for free all along the promenade, actually consists of three falls – Horseshoe Falls, the American Falls, and the Bridal Veil Falls, that straddle the international border between Canada and the US. Niagara Falls is also the namesake city in which the falls reside, and it's a tacky but colorful city with too many casinos, sleazy motels, and tourist traps.

The views of the falls are, thankfully, best appreciated from the Canadian side, and are at their wildest in the late spring and early summer. The Horseshoe Falls

A wet experience

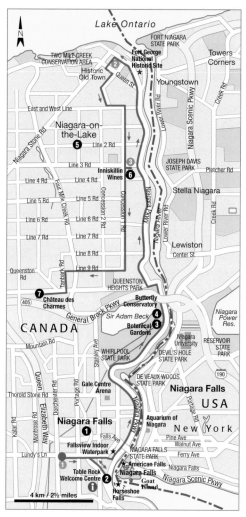

are the mightiest and are 57 meters (188ft) high, and 790 meters (2,600ft) wide. During the winter, ice formations on the falls are quite spectacular and the crowds have disappeared. The falls are illuminated in a rainbow of colors every evening, from dusk until late, certainly one reason to stick around for a night. Fireworks shows, right above the falls, are held nightly beginning at 10pm in the summer, then just on weekends and special holidays throughout the rest of the year.

There are many ways to experience the falls. Board one of the **Hornblower Cruises** (tel: 1-855-264-2427; daily May–Nov; www.niagaracruises.com) to get up close to the falls, feel the mist, and hear the thundering roar, as this boat trip takes you on a 700-passenger vessel right into the heart of the falls. Prices include a mist poncho as you will get wet.

For a self-guided walk alongside the rapids, there's the **White Water Walk** (daily mid-Apr–early Nov). Or to see

A fine specimen at the Butterfly Conservatory

them from above you can board the **Whirlpool Aero Car**, a historic cable car offering spectacular views and a ride children will particularly enjoy. You can even zip-line across the rapids; all details are on the website.

King Tours (tel: 416-315-4065; www.kingtours.ca) is one of the top tour companies that has daily departures from Toronto to Niagara Falls. Tours are for the full day and guests are picked up from their hotel in the morning. Stops include Niagara-on-the-Lake and a winery visits and tasting. Add-ons can be included, such as a lunch or a cruise tour.

TABLE ROCK WELCOME CENTRE

A visit to the **Table Rock Welcome Centre ❷** (tel: 905-358-3268; www.niagaraparks.com; Mon–Fri 9am–5pm, Sat–Sun 9am–8pm) is a good starting point when arriving in the city of Niagara Falls. Located right at the falls, this complex has several attractions, such as Niagara's Fury, a 4D simulation of the creation of the falls, and the Journey Behind the Falls, where visitors descend down 46 meters (151ft) by elevator and get in behind and below the falls. The center also has a food court, gift shops, and an information booth. For a quick bite to eat, especially if breakfast was skipped or hurried that morning, pop into the **Flying Saucer**, see ❶, about 10 minutes drive west of the center, and it's as crazy as it sounds.

BOTANICAL GARDENS & BUTTERFLY CONSERVATORY

Established in 1936, the **Botanical Gardens ❸** (tel: 905-356-8119; www.niagaraparks.com; daily, dawn until dusk; free) consists of over 40 hectares (100 acres) of beautifully landscaped gardens filled with roses, herbs, and manicured hedges. The **Butterfly Conservatory ❹** (tel: 905-358-0025; www.niagaraparks.com; daily 10am–7pm) is located within the gardens and transports visitors to a tropical paradise full of lush plants, misty waterfalls, and thousands of free-flying butterflies.

Niagara facts

- The falls are only about 10,000 years old, created by glacial activity during the last ice age.
- American daredevil Nik Wallenda crossed the falls on a tightrope in 2012, the first person to do this since 1896. The very first person to successfully cross was professional French tightrope walker Charles Blondin, who did it in 1859.
- The first person to go over the falls, and survive, was 63-year-old Annie Edson Taylor, who used a custom-made oak and iron barrel.
- The Horseshoe Falls have frozen over just once, but the American Falls have frozen over six times.

Niagara-on-the-Lake

NIAGARA-ON-THE-LAKE

Located on the shores of Lake Ontario, the charming town of **Niagara-on-the-Lake** ❺ is just 23km (14 miles) north of Niagara Falls. Less kitschy than Niagara Falls, it's famous for its wineries, well-preserved colonial-style buildings, and numerous heritage sites. Niagara-on-the-Lake is also home to the annual Shaw Festival, a major theater event featuring the plays of George Bernard Shaw as well as works by other writers, which runs from April to October.

For lunch, enjoy true farm-to-table fare at **Treadwell Cuisine**, see ❷.

INNISKILLIN WINES AND CHÂTEAU DES CHARMES

Heading back out from Niagara-on-the-Lake, stop at the **Inniskillin Wines** ❻ (tel: 905-468-2187; www.inniskillin.com; daily 10am–6pm May–Oct, Mon–Sat 10am–5pm Nov–Apr; free tours), a historic and pioneering winery famous for its ice wine and range of table wines. Inniskillin also has a seasonal eatery, serving smoked and grilled meats for lunch at the **Market Grill & Smokehouse,** see ❸.

Before heading back to Toronto, visit the winery of **Château des Charmes** ❼ (tel: 905-262-4219; www.fromtheboscfamily.com; daily 10am–6pm). Known for its chardonnay, this winery has gorgeous grounds to stroll around.

Food and Drink

❶ FLYING SAUCER
6768 Lundy's Lane; tel: 905-356-4553; www.flyingsaucerrestaurant.com; daily B, L, and D; $
Cheap and incredibly cheerful, this is not just a touristy, sci-fi themed diner – the locals love it too, especially the kids. The early-bird breakfast special here is just $3 with the purchase of a drink, and includes two eggs, home fries, and toast.

❷ TREADWELL CUISINE
114 Queen Street; tel: 905-934-9797; www.treadwellcuisine.com; daily L and D; $$$
This classy but relaxed restaurant proudly showcases fresh, seasonal, and local ingredients through its delectable Canadian menu. The Lobster Club sandwich with duck fat and sun-dried tomato whipped goat cheese is incredible. They have a bakery across the lane too.

❸ MARKET GRILL & SMOKEHOUSE
1499 Line 3 Niagara Parkway; tel: 905-468-2187; www.inniskillin.com; 11am–4pm daily July–Sept 3, May–June and 4 Sept–Oct Sat–Sun only; $$
Poutines, grilled and smoked meats, sandwiches, salads, and oysters are on the seasonal menu at this picturesque lunch spot. Try the Inniskillin Ice Cream Sandwich for dessert – a double chocolate brownie with vanilla ice cream, topped with a non-alcoholic Cabernet Franc syrup.

DIRECTORY

Hand-picked hotels and restaurants to suit all budgets and tastes, organized by area, plus select nightlife listings, an alphabetical listing of practical information, and an overview of the best books and films to give you a flavor of the city.

The lofty interior of the Fairmont Royal York

ACCOMMODATIONS

From peaceful bed and breakfasts and conventional hotels and motels, to luxurious landmark properties, Toronto offers plenty of choice for accommodations in a range of needs and budgets. Prices are relatively high, however, but this is a major city, after all.

Most of the hotels are centered around Downtown, with some decent options near the airport and surrounding neighborhoods. Accommodations usually always offer complimentary WiFi, but parking and breakfast are generally not included.

Reservations are essential in the busy summer months. Hotels will usually hold a room until 6pm, but if you plan to arrive later, notify the establishment in advance. If you have not reserved, begin looking for accommodations early in the afternoon, particularly in peak seasons when most establishments fill up quickly.

All hotels, motels, and resorts accept major credit cards, and all are completely smoke-free. Although the price ranges quoted are for the lowest current rack rate at the time of going to press, ask about special packages and promotions when making a reservation. Off-season rates can be much lower. The prices indicated are based on double occupancy.

Price for a standard double room for one night, excluding taxes and breakfast, in high season.
$$$$ = over $400
$$$ = $250–400
$$ = $150–250
$ = less than $150

City Center

The Adelaide Hotel
325 Bay Street; tel: 416-306-5800; www.adelaidehoteltoronto.com; $$$
This chic hotel is right in the center of it all, with suites that include gas fireplaces, wet bars, and soaker tubs. The heated indoor saltwater pool on the 32nd floor has wide views of the Toronto skyline.

The Anndore House
15 Charles Street East; tel: 416-924-1222; www.theanndorehouse.com; $$$
Industrial with an Art Deco vibe, this 11-story brick boutique hotel features rooms that resemble a hip designer's space complete with exposed brick walls, leather chairs, subway-tiled bathrooms, and vinyl record players. The lovely hotel restaurant, Constantine, has a Mediterranean-focused menu that can be enjoyed all day, notably for brunch.

Bisha Hotel
80 Blue Jays Way; tel: 416-551-2800; www.bishahoteltoronto.com; $$$

Feminine touches at The Ivy at Verity

At the epicenter of the Entertainment District, this chic and lush hotel is filled with artworks and even has an entire floor designed by rocker Lenny Kravitz. The rooftop patio and outdoor infinity pool offer stunning views of Downtown.

Chelsea Hotel

33 Gerrard Street West; tel: 416-595-1975; www.chelseatoronto.com; $$

This is Canada's largest hotel, and it is very family-friendly with a special KidZone, two indoor swimming pools, an indoor water slide, an arcade room, and several eateries to choose from. The Family Fun Suites come with an Xbox and other nice toys.

Courtyard Toronto Downtown

475 Yonge Street; tel: 416-924-0611; marriott.com; $$

Polished and good value, this modern, centrally located hotel keeps it simple and practical. Some rooms have balconies with city views, and the fitness center is open 24hrs.

Delta Hotels by Marriott Toronto

75 Lower Simcoe Street; tel: 416-849-1200; www.marriott.com; $$

Lake and island views and plenty of perks can be found at this modern, pet-friendly high-rise hotel. Extended stay options are available here as well, with suites that have full kitchens. The onsite Char No. 5 Whiskey Bar offers evening snacks and cocktails.

Fairmont Royal York

100 Front Street West; tel: 416-368-2511; www.fairmont.com; $$

Historic, château-style, landmark hotel that's conveniently linked with the PATH underground walkway system. It's full of old-world charm but still very family-friendly with babysitting services, a children's wading pool, and cribs on request.

Hilton Toronto

145 Richmond Street West; tel: 416-869-3456; www3.hilton.com; $$

Connected to the PATH underground walkway system, this large business hotel has a lovely heated indoor/outdoor pool with a bar, and the suites are suitable for extended stays.

HI Toronto

76 Church Street; tel: 416-971-4440; www.hostellingtoronto.com; $

Lively hostel with simple shared rooms or private rooms with ensuite bathrooms. A breakfast voucher is included and can be used at the onsite Cavern Bar, which gets busy in the evenings so the hostel also provides free earplugs. Barbecues are held on the rooftop patio, weather permitting.

The Ivy at Verity

111 Queen Street East; tel: 416-368-6006; www.theivyatverity.com; $$$$

Geared toward female travelers, this opulent boutique hotel is located in a restored 1850s chocolate factory and

The Consort Bar at the Omni King Edward Hotel

features just four exquisitely decorated rooms with private terraces. Continental breakfast is included and delivered right to your room.

Hotel Le Germain Maple Leaf Square

75 Bremner Boulevard; tel: 888-940-7575; www.legermainhotels.com; $$$

Located right on Maple Leaf Square, just a few steps from the Scotiabank Arena, this modern, luxury hotel is perfect for the sports fan. The 24hr fitness center is fantastic, too.

The Omni King Edward Hotel

37 King Street East; tel: 416-863-9700; www.omnihotels.com; $$$

Built in 1903 as the first luxury hotel in Toronto, the Omni King Edward has kept its historic ambiance but combines it elegantly with modern updates. Try the classic afternoon tea served in Victoria's Restaurant.

One King West Hotel & Residence

1 King Street West; tel: 416-548-8100; www.onekingwest.com; $$$

Upscale and grand all-suite hotel converted from the historic 19th-century Toronto Dominion Bank building, with much of the structure's original character still preserved. The rooms are contemporary however, and all have well-appointed kitchenettes.

The Planet Traveler Hostel

357 College Street; tel: 647-699-5647; www.theplanettraveler.com; $

Inside a restored historic brick building this hostel has a choice of basic shared dorm-style or private rooms. A free and unlimited breakfast is included, and the rooftop patio with its solar-paneled roof has amazing city skyline views.

The Ritz-Carlton

181 Wellington Street West; tel: 416-585-2500; www.ritzcarlton.com; $$$$

Expect high-end, spacious rooms with impressive marble bathrooms complete with TVs in the mirrors, plus heated floors, at this large Ritz hotel. The full-service spa and Italian Toca restaurant are excellent as well.

The Saint James Hotel

26 Gerrard Street East; tel: 416-645-2200; www.thesaintjameshotel.com; $$$

Good value hotel, right next to Ryerson University, with bright, clean rooms featuring hardwood floors and Keurig coffee makers. Breakfast is complimentary and guests receive a little welcome goody bag upon arrival.

A Seaton Dream B&B

243 Seaton Street; tel: 416-929-3363; www.aseatondream.com; $$

A welcoming bed and breakfast in a Victorian-era townhouse with three guest rooms that offer ensuite bathrooms, fine traditional decor, and hardwood floors. A hot breakfast and parking are included.

The Windsor Arms Hotel

Shangri-La Hotel Toronto

188 University Avenue; tel: 647-788-8888;
www.shangri-la.com; $$$$

Luxury high-rise hotel located right in the Financial District, featuring elegant Asian-inspired decor, suites with butler service, and a huge, 24-hour fitness center that includes a yoga studio. The vibrant lobby has live music every evening.

SoHo Metropolitan

318 Wellington Street West; tel: 416-599-8800; www.metropolitan.com; $$$

Popular with visiting celebrities, this relaxed, boutique hotel has a complimentary luxury sedan service and an upscale all-day dim sum eatery. The top-notch fitness center even comes with a personal trainer.

Templar Hotel

348 Adelaide Street West; tel: 416-479-0847; www.templarhotel.com; $$

Located right in the Fashion District, this architect-owned boutique hotel has ultra contemporary rooms featuring huge bathrooms, floor-to-ceiling windows, and hardwood and stone floors. While here, try the excellent pizza at the General Assembly across the street.

Windsor Arms Hotel

18 St Thomas Street; tel: 416-971-9666;
www.windsorarmshotel.com; $$$$

Opulent boutique hotel from the 1920s with period decor and modern amenities such as Nespresso machines. The suites even include a musical instrument to use. The indoor saltwater pool is lovely, and the location is in Toronto's prime shopping district, Bloor-Yorkville.

Midtown

Clinton and Bloor Bed & Breakfast

390 Clinton Street; tel: 416-538-0417;
www.clintonandbloor.com; $$

Conveniently located in Koreatown, and right by the Christie subway station, this friendly B&B has three contemporary suites with ensuite bathrooms. A delicious hot breakfast is included in the rate.

Four Seasons Hotel Toronto

60 Yorkville Avenue; tel: 416-964-0411;
www.fourseasons.com; $$$$

One of the city's best hotels, offering the epitome of modern luxury. Guest rooms are bright and feature signature Four Seasons beds with down duvets and pillows. There's an onsite Michelin-starred restaurant, an exquisite spa, and an ultra-modern fitness center with a yoga studio and pool.

The Hazelton Hotel

118 Yorkville Avenue; tel: 416-963-6300;
www.thehazeltonhotel.com; $$$$

Luxurious and pet-friendly boutique property with spacious guest rooms that include heated granite floors and rainfall showers in the bathrooms. The indoor saltwater pool is small but amazing, and the classy lobby bar serves up fabulous cocktails.

Quirky accents at The Drake Hotel

InterContinental Toronto Yorkville

220 Bloor Street West; tel: 416-960-5200;
www.toronto.intercontinental.com; $$

Relaxed and comfortable hotel in The Annex with one of best cocktail bars in the neighborhood, Proof. It has a lovely courtyard patio for the warmer months.

Kimpton Saint George

280 Bloor Street West; tel: 416-968-0010;
www.kimptonsaintgeorge.com; $$$

A luxury boutique hotel featuring a vintage color palette and modern furnishings. Rooms come with record players and yoga mats. Complimentary bikes are available, too, plus there's a wine hour each evening, a 24-hour fitness center, and a lively gastropub onsite.

Eastside

The Broadview

106 Broadview Avenue; tel: 416-362-8439;
www.thebroadviewhotel.ca; $$$

With roots dating back to 1891, this historic building in the up-and-coming Leslieville neighborhood was long known as the location of a popular strip club, but that notorious affiliation will be short-lived. The building has been completely transformed into a luxury boutique hotel with beautiful, individually unique rooms, and a fabulous rooftop bar and restaurant.

Westside

Annex Garden Bed & Breakfast

445 Euclid Avenue; tel: 647-696-7669;
www.annexgarden.com; $$

Charming B&B in the Little Italy neighborhood, on a former estate from 1885. The Victorian and Edwardian architectural features of the house have been carefully restored, and modern amenities have been added. Rooms and suites are luxurious with fireplaces and

Boutique chic at the Kimpton Saint George

The Gladstone Hotel

ensuite bathrooms, and rates include breakfast and parking.

By The Park Bed & Breakfast

92 Indian Grove; tel: 416-520-6102; www.bythepark.ca; $$

Well-established, spotless, and sophisticated bed and breakfast comprising of two heritage houses, one with four suites that includes a vegetarian breakfast, the other with five self-catering suites. All suites include parking, some have fireplaces and full kitchens.

The Drake Hotel

1150 Queen Street West; tel: 416-531-5042; www.thedrake.ca; $$$

Trendy and artsy boutique hotel in the lively Arts and Design District. Guest rooms are colorful, contemporary, and unique – a mixture of ultra luxurious and kitsch/bizarre, from the handcrafted furniture and big beds through to the peculiar dolls left on the pillows. With multiple restaurants and bars onsite, there's always an event happening here, from an art show to live music.

Gladstone Hotel

1214 Queen Street West; tel: 416-531-4635; www.gladstonehotel.com; $$

Housed in a handsome Victorian brick building, this hipster-cool, art-focused boutique hotel has 37 unique rooms to choose from, all designed by different local artists. Perks include free bike rentals, yoga classes, and frequent art exhibits. The communal areas serve as art galleries and, as this is the most fashionable part of town, the hotel bar heaves, so forget it if you're after a quiet night – people come here to razzle it up.

Old Mill Toronto

9 Old Mill Road; tel: 416-232-3707; www.oldmilltoronto.com; $$

For a romantic getaway just outside of downtown, this elegant English-Tudor-style property right along the Humber River is just perfect. The spacious rooms include four-poster beds, Jacuzzi tubs, and stunning views of the lush grounds and surrounding Humber Valley.

Thompson Hotel Toronto

550 Wellington Street West; tel: 416-640-7778; www.thompsonhotels.com; $$$

Chic and hip boutique hotel featuring gorgeous, modern rooms with luxurious marble bathrooms. Check out the lively rooftop bar and infinity pool with amazing city and lake vistas and excellent cocktails and tapas.

Waterfront

Making Waves Boatel

539 Queens Way West; tel: 647-403-2764; www.boatel.ca; $$$

Docked at Marina Quay West, this 20-meter (65ft) private yacht is yours for the night, breakfast included. All three guest rooms can be booked or just one or two of them, it's up to you, with a choice of an ensuite or shared bathroom.

The Cadillac Motel, straight out of a movie

Radisson Admiral Toronto Harbourfront

249 Queen's Quay West; tel: 416-203-3333; www.radisson.com; $$

Stylish, harborfront hotel, yet still close enough to Downtown and its attractions. Rooms have hardwood floors and excellent CN Tower and lake views, and some even have gas fireplaces. The large outdoor pool and patio are lively during the summer months.

Hotel X Toronto

111 Princes Boulevard; tel: 647-943-9300; www.hotelxtoronto.com; $$$$

Chic and modern resort-style hotel with unparalleled waterfront and city skyline views, multiple dining options, a kids play center, four indoor tennis courts, nine squash courts, and a gorgeous rooftop pool.

The Westin Harbour Castle Hotel

1 Harbour Square; tel: 416-869-1600; www.marriott.com; $$$

Two 34-story waterfront towers make up this urban modern resort, complete with a large fitness center, an indoor pool, tennis courts, full service spa, and various eateries to choose from. It's also family and pet friendly, with special amenities and services for both.

Airport

Best Western Plus Travel Hotel Toronto Airport

5503 Eglinton Avenue West; tel: 416-620-1234; www.bestwestern.com; $

A practical option for staying close to the Toronto Pearson International Airport, this business hotel has clean, comfortable rooms, a small fitness center, a complimentary airport shuttle, and a complimentary breakfast.

Homewood Suites by Hilton Toronto Airport Corporate Centre

5515 Eglinton Avenue West; tel: 416-646-4600; www.hilton.com; $$

Convenient airport location for short and long-term stays, with large, modern suites that include a fully equipped kitchen. Other extras include an onsite 24-hour convenience store, fitness center, indoor pool, and a courtyard with a barbecue area and even a putting green.

Outside of Toronto

Abacot Hall Bed & Breakfast

508 Mississauga Street, Niagara-on-the-Lake; tel: 905-468-8383; www.abacothall.com; $$

Well-run, friendly bed & breakfast in an elegant, Georgian-style home surrounded by manicured gardens. Each of the ensuite rooms has been beautifully decorated and has air conditioning. There's also a delightful cook-to-order breakfast.

The Butler House Historic Bed & Breakfast

67 Mary Street, Niagara-on-the-Lake; tel: 905-468-9696; www.thebutlerhouse.ca; $$

A suite at the Queens Landing Hotel

Romantic bed & breakfast with an English country charm set in a property dating back to 1814. Rooms are beautifully decorated and feature all modern facilities. Breakfast is a gourmet, three-course endeavor.

Cadillac Motel

5342 Ferry Street, Niagara Falls; tel: 905-356-0830; www.cadillacmotelniagara.com; $

Built in 1957, this famous motel has featured in quite a few Hollywood movies. Today, the modest and trendy retro-style rooms include private bathrooms, a microwave, a mini-fridge, air conditioning, and free parking. The falls are just two blocks away.

Harbour House Hotel

85 Melville Street, Niagara-on-the-Lake; tel: 289-806-0223; www.niagarasfinest.com; $$$

Historic and charming waterfront property located in the center of town, with bright, luxurious rooms that feature down duvets, gas fireplaces, a complimentary breakfast as well as afternoon wine tastings.

Queen's Landing

155 Byron Street, Niagara-on-the-Lake; tel: 905-468-2195; www.vintage-hotels.com; $$$

Across the street from the Harbor House Hotel, this Georgian-style stately hotel was actually built in 1990 but on the site of the Old Niagara Harbour and Dock Company from 1831. There are four special Dockmasters Suites located in the historic annex of the dock company that are true pinnacles of luxury.

The Rex Motel

6247 McLeod Road, Niagara Falls; tel: 289-807-2723; www.rexmotel.com; $

For a budget-friendly option, this small, family-run motel in a quiet neighborhood has colorful and clean rooms, offers free parking, and has an outdoor play area for kids.

Shaw Club Hotel

92 Picton Street, Niagara-on-the-Lake; tel: 289-273-5111; www.niagarasfinest.com; $$

Designed to feel like a private hotel, though it is part of a chain, this contemporary property features luxurious rooms with gas fireplaces, down duvets, and even a pet fish if you wish. Parking is complimentary as is the shuttle service for around town.

Sterling Inn & Spa

5195 Magdalen Street, Niagara Falls; tel: 289-292-0000; www.sterlingniagara.com; $$

The spacious rooms of this modern hotel boast four-poster beds, hardwood floors, fireplaces, and steam-shower bathrooms. A lovely continental breakfast is delivered to your room each morning. The onsite AG restaurant (see page 100) is a real highlight.

RESTAURANTS

Toronto's dining scene is wonderfully varied and exciting, mainly due to the diversity of its residents, but also thanks to the incredibly talented chefs that call this city home. Price ranges, too, are across the board, suiting every budget.

From authentic Chinese dim sum, to Italian pizzas and American barbecue, flavors are truly global in this city. Sometimes the choices can be a bit overwhelming, so simple sandwiches and salads are always available at cafés and casual eateries. Fancy tasting menus abound, however, if that's what you're looking for.

In any case, foodies, and even those just searching for a filling meal, will not be disappointed. Just be sure to make reservations, if available, for any special restaurants that you may want to try, and a 15–20 percent tip is customary if the service was good. Also, in Toronto people typically eat dinner at about 7pm, which is when you'll notice restaurants beginning to fill up. If you didn't make any reservations, arriving prior to this time may allow you to secure a spot after all.

City Center

Aloette

163 Spadina Avenue; tel: 416-260-3444; www.aloetterestaurant.com; daily L and D; $$$

Elegant and sleek French bistro with a diner feel, located on the ground level of the same building as its fine-dining sister Alo, upstairs. The menu is simple but special with fantastic beef carpaccio and foie gras terrine, and a notable house burger. Aloette doesn't take reservations, so come early.

Beast

96 Tecumseth Street; tel: 647-352-6000; www.thebeastrestaurant.com; L and D Wed–Sun; $$

Tucked away on a quiet residential street, Beast is considered a meat-focused restaurant, but it's really all about the biscuits (buns) here – specifically, the biscuit sandwiches. House-made, buttermilk-rich, and super soft and flaky, at brunch time they can be filled with a choice of eggs, fried chicken, peameal bacon, smoked brisket, or even just served with a luscious gravy.

Buca

604 King Street West; tel: 416-865-1600; www.buca.ca; daily D; $$$

> Price for a two-course meal for one including a glass of wine (or other beverage)
> $$$$ = over $60
> $$$ = $45–60
> $$ = $20–-45
> $ = under $20

Burger and fries at Chubby's Jamaican Kitchen

Rustic Italian fare, including house-made charcuterie, fresh pastas, and pizzas, served efficiently in an always crowded, modern, dimly-lit space. If you're looking for more of a cocktail and shared plates kind of spot, head over to equally great Bar Buca, just a block south.

Byblos

11 Duncan Street; tel: 647-660-0909; www. byblostoronto.com; $$$

Saffron, anise, za'atar, and other exotic spices and fragrances of Eastern Mediterranean cuisine come alive here, with a choice of a bright and airy main floor for seating or a more sultry lounge upstairs. To start, try the duck kibbeh appetizer, followed by the short rib kebab, a fatoush salad, and, to finish, the orange blossom mousse.

Bymark

66 Wellington Street West; tel: 416-777-1144; www.bymark.mcewangroup.ca; Mon–Fri L and D, Sat D; $$$$

There's much more to this suit and tie restaurant than the famous, and also amazing, $40 burger, even if it comes served with shaved truffles and brie cheese. The new Canadian cuisine crafted and presented here is utterly fantastic. Try their take on the classic poutine – with butter-braised lobster.

Chubby's Jamaican Kitchen

104 Portland Street; tel: 416-792-8105; www. chubbysjamaican.com; daily L and D; $$

Be temporarily transported to the tropics, with a retro-resort decor, papaya salads, sizzling meats on the grill, and cocktails served inside pineapples. Finish the meal with a passion fruit coconut cream pie to complete the experience.

Hibiscus Café

238 Augusta Avenue; tel: 416-364-6183; www.hibiscuscafe.ca; Tue–Sun L; $$

Family-run vegetarian café in the heart of Kensington Market. The savory and sweet buckwheat crepes are their best sellers, but the homemade dairy-free ice cream served in gluten-free cones are incredible, too.

Jacobs & Co. Steakhouse

12 Brandt Street; tel: 416-366-0200; www. jacobssteakhouse.com; daily D; $$$$

An elegant steakhouse for those special occasions, with white linens, first-rate service, and even a piano bar. Caesar salad is prepared table side, the steak menu is according to its origin – from local to Japanese beef – and the wine list is incredibly extensive with nearly 1,000 labels to choose from.

Jumbo Empanadas

245 Augusta Avenue; tel: 416-977-0056; www.jumboempanadas.ca; daily L; $

Authentic Chilean comfort food, specializing specifically in empanadas – warm pastry pockets filled with your choice of vegetables, cheese, chicken, or beef.

Kojin is all about local ingredients

Kid Lee

100 King Street West; tel: 647-352-0092;
Mon–Thu 11am–6pm, Fri 9am–4pm; $
Located inside First Canadian Place's upstairs dining area, this healthy food court serves up generous portions of hearty and absolutely mouth-watering Singaporean-fusion dishes. The tropical juices are refreshing and come in convenient take-out bottles, or ask for a freshly cut coconut drink.

King Place

236 Sherbourne Street; tel: 647-352-0786;
no website; daily L and D; $
Open until 6am, this Pakistani take-out joint in the Cabbagetown neighborhood is ideal for those wee hours. If you do take-out, they serve it cold unless you ask for it warmed up. Choose from fragrant chicken, hearty beef or vegetarian curries, rice dishes, fresh naan bread, and exotic desserts.

King's Noodle Restaurant

296 Spadina Avenue; tel: 416-598-1817;
www.kingsnoodle.ca; Thu–Tue B, L, and
D; $
Traditional Chinatown restaurant complete with roasted duck and pork hanging in the window. Don't expect stellar service here, but do expect delicious barbecued duck, fried dough fritters, and fresh noodle dishes. This is a cash only establishment.

Kinka Izakaya

398 Church Street; tel: 416-977-0999;
www.kinka.com; daily L and D; $$
Loud and fun Japanese pub with delicious small plates to share and lots of drinks to choose from. This is a perfect spot for an adventurous group looking to try some unusual dishes or go for the set menu to play it relatively safe.

Kojin

190 University Avenue; tel: 647-253-6227;
https://kojin.momofuku.com; L Mon–Fri,
daily D; $$$
Part of the global Momofuku restaurant brand, this stunning Canadian cuisine-focused restaurant harnesses the best local produce, seafood, and meats available, and uses a wood-fire grill for much of the cooking.

Kupfert & Kim

140 Spadina Avenue; tel: 416-504-2206;
www.kupfertandkim.com; B, L, and D daily; $$
'Wheatless and meatless' is the proud slogan of this small, local fast-food chain. But don't think this translates as tasteless – this little take-out spot is excellent; everything is made in-house using mostly organic, local ingredients. The cauliflower tahini bowl is a must-try, with quinoa, hummus, a za'atar salsa, and fresh veggies.

Los Colibris

220 King Street West; tel: 647-560-8277;
www.loscolibris.ca; Mon–Sat D; $$$
Located above its sister restaurant, El Caballito, the more refined, white linen Los Colibris is focused less on street

A salad at Rasa

food and more on traditional Mexican recipes. Fresh shrimp ceviche, succulent braised pork shoulder, and quite a few vegetarian options are on the menu here.

Mira

420A Wellington Street West; tel: 647-951-3331; www.mirarestaurant.com; daily D; $$
Colorful and contemporary Peruvian restaurant and bar with exotic small plates of traditional and fusion bites such as yuca fries, beef tartare, and lobster-topped rice. For dessert, the El Huevo Malo – essentially a giant chocolate Easter egg surprise, is not to be missed.

Pearl Diver

100 Adelaide Street East; tel: 416-366-7827; www.pearldiver.to; Thu–Sun L and D, Mon–Wed D; $$
Relaxed seafood bar specializing in fresh oysters. Of course shrimp cocktails, chowders, and fish and chips are on the menu as well. Try the Seafood Tower for a bit of everything, and the summer takeout window is great for quick picnic orders.

Pow Wow Café

213 Augusta Avenue; tel: 416-551-7717; no website; daily L and D; $$
Tacos, Ojibway-style, using frybread at this Indigenous Canadian-inspired eatery. There are four choices – beef chili, veggie chili, coconut lime chicken curry, and pork souvlaki. Each taco is generously portioned and absolutely delicious.

Rasa

196 Robert Street; tel: 647-350-8221; www.rasabar.ca; L Sun, Mon–Sat D; $$
Subterranean, industrial-chic space dishing up globally inspired and creatively plated tapas such as empanadas, ceviche, steak tartare, and roasted lamb. The cocktails are equally creative – enjoy one or two outside in the heated, street-level patio.

The Senator

249 Victoria Street; tel: 416-364-7517; www.thesenator.com; daily B and L, Tue–Sat D; $$
Possibly the city's oldest restaurant, housed in a building dating back to the 1850s, this classic diner serves up comfort foods daily, but it's best known for its weekend brunch.

Tinuno

31 Howard Street; tel: 647-343-9294; www.tinunothirtyone.com; daily B, L, and D; $$
Bright and simple small space with mouthwatering traditional Filipino specialties, all from the grill. Try the Kamayan Feast, which is served on a banana leaf with sticky rice, and meant to eat with your hands. It includes an assortment of grilled seafood, meat, and vegetables.

Midtown

Jacques Bistro du Parc

126 Cumberland Street; tel: 416-961-1893; www.jacquesbistro.com; Tue–Sat L and D; $$$
Locals have happily dined inside this tiny fine French restaurant since the late

Simple but delicious fare awaits at Dandylion

1970s, and luckily not a whole lot has changed since then. The refined menu is served in an unpretentious manner and offers classics such as onion soup, escargots, pâtés, mussels, and specialty fresh fish dishes.

Planta

1221 Bay Street; tel: 647-348-7000; www.plantarestaurants.com; L and D daily; $$$

As the name suggests, all the dishes served in this bright, modern vegan restaurant are plant-based. And they are no ordinary dishes. Menu items include beautifully plated coconut ceviche, matcha soba noodles, tomato tarts, gourmet pizzas, and eggplant lasagna, to name a few.

Pukka

778 St Clair Avenue West; tel: 416-342-1906; www.pukka.ca; D daily; $$$

Modern Indian restaurant with an excellent wine list. The menu offers shareable and creative bar snacks, comforting curries using local ingredients such as wild sockeye salmon and Quebec duck breast, and for dessert there's sticky toffee pudding and pavlova.

Westside

416 Snack Bar

181 Bathurst Street; tel: 416-364-9320; www.416snackbar.com; L and D Fri–Sun, D Mon–Thu; $$

Late-night casual eatery serving up an eclectic global menu of shareable small plates. The dishes are meant to reflect Toronto's wonderful diversity so expect Korean fried chicken, steamed pork buns, spicy tuna rolls, pakoras, falafel, oysters, and more.

Bar Isabel

797 College Street; tel: 416-532-2222; www.barisabel.com; daily D; $$$

Lively but intimate Spanish tapas tavern with delicious small plates on offer for sharing, including cheeses, meats, and seafood specialties. The cocktail and wine lists are excellent, too, and for a fee you can bring in your own bottle of wine if you wish.

Boralia

59 Ossington Avenue; tel: 647-351-5100; www.boraliato.com; Wed–Sun D; $$$

Celebrating the historic origins of Canadian cuisine, Boralia's menu is inspired by Aboriginal dishes, as well as recipes from early pioneers of the 18th and 19th centuries. Venison, arctic char, and pigeon are just some of the main ingredients used in the creative offerings here.

Café Polonez

195 Roncesvalles Avenue; tel: 416-532-8432; www.cafepolonez.ca; daily L and D; $$

Rightfully located in the heart of the city's Polish community, this inviting, established family-run restaurant serves up hearty portions of Eastern European favorites such as borscht, potato pancakes, goulash, pierogies, and schnitzel. There's a good selection of Polish beers and vodka as well.

Boralia restaurant   *Chefs at work at Grey Gardens*

DaiLo

503 College Street; tel: 647-341-8882; www.dailoto.com; Tue–Sun D; $$$

Contemporary and fun Chinese-fusion restaurant with a cool cocktail bar upstairs. The eclectic menu includes pumpkin dumplings, fried winter melon, and jellyfish slaw. Go for the Chef's Menu for the best selection if you're unsure.

Dandylion

1198 Queen Street West; tel: 647-464-9100; www.restaurantdandylion.com; Tue–Sat D; $$$

Cozy, narrow space with an exposed-brick décor and an open kitchen. The ever-changing and modest Canadian menu is unusual, in that it only lists a handful of ingredients from each dish, so it's a bit of a surprise what arrives at the table, but always a delight.

Doma

50 Clinton Street; tel: 416-551-1550; www.domatoronto.com; Tue–Sat D; $$$

Little Italy isn't just about Italian restaurants. Doma, a modern Korean-French fusion restaurant, is a perfect example. Dishes are artfully plated here, and offer unusual combination of flavors, such as the traditional Korean bibimbap made with black rice and truffles.

Enoteca Sociale

1288 Dundas Street West; tel: 416-534-1200; www.sociale.ca; daily D; $$$

Quaint and friendly trattoria serving fine cheeses, cured meats, house-made bread, and fresh pastas. The wine list is fantastic, and there's even a real cheese cave in the basement.

Foxley

207 Ossington Avenue; tel: 416-534-8520; no website; Mon–Sat D; $$$

Casual little Asian-fusion tapas bar known for its ceviche and cocktails. During the summer months, their patio is just perfect. They don't take reservations so, since it's a small place, you'll want to come early to get a spot.

Grand Electric

1330 Queen Street West; tel: 416-627-3459; www.grandelectrictoronto.com; daily L and D; $$

Local, vibrant, and loud hang-out for creative Mexican fare, such as tacos, quesadillas, and tostadas, served at communal tables. Their unusual take on key lime pie is wonderfully delicious.

Grey Gardens

199 Augusta Avenue; tel: 647-351-1552; www.greygardens.ca; D daily; $$$

Bright and fresh, with an open kitchen and a vintage feel, this place doubles as a terrific wine bar in the late evenings. Featuring a new North American menu, pick from creative vegetarian dishes, fresh seafood, steak, pasta, and scrumptious desserts.

Hanmoto

2 Lakeview Avenue; no phone or website; D Mon–Sat; $$

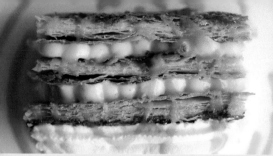

Mille-feuille at La Palma

Japanese dive bar with a kitchen that stays open till 2am offering a range of filling and superbly flavorful snack items. Try the decadent Katsu Bun, the Dyno wings (essentially stuffed chicken wings), or the Nasu Dengaku, a deep fried eggplant dish with a miso hollandaise sauce and fried shredded beets.

The Hogtown Vegan

1056 Bloor Street West; tel: 416-901-9779; www.hogtownvegan.com; L and D daily; $$
Comfort vegan food with a 'southern' twist. The reuben sandwich is made with a pumpernickel rye, layered with sauerkraut, meatless strips, plus a spicy mayo and garlic butter, or try the unchicken and waffles, made with breaded tofu and served with fluffy corn waffles.

Imanishi Japanese Kitchen

1330 Dundas Street West; tel: 416-706-4225; www.imanishi.ca; daily D; $$
Cozy, Japanese home-cooking eatery with a Tokyo-Inspired menu. Choose from such items as fresh sashimi, beef tataki, curried rice dishes, and speciality set meals. Note that the small signage outside of this eatery is easy to miss.

La Banane

227 Ossington Avenue; tel: 416-551-6263; www.labanane.ca; daily D; $$$$
Modern French seafood bistro and raw bar with creative dishes on the menu, including the beautifully presented eurobass en croûte. For dessert, don't miss the Ziggy Stardust Disco Egg – a chocolate egg made with apricots, ancho chillies, and coffee beans, and filled with chocolate truffles.

La Cubana

92 Ossington Avenue; tel: 416-537-0134; www.lacubana.ca; daily noon–10pm, Fri–Sat until midnight; $$
Fresh and cool lunchtime favorite on the Ossington Strip, featuring an amazing pressed Cubano sandwich made with thinly sliced ham, sous-vide pork shoulder, gruyère cheese, and some condiments. The Guava BBQ Short Rib is fantastic as well, with a side of Yuca Frita – crispy fried cassava root.

La Palma

849 Dundas Street West; tel: 416-368-4567; www.lapalma.ca; daily L and D, Sat–Sun B; $$$
Bright and airy northern Italian eatery and take-out counter with a beachy California vibe. Try the 100-layer lasagna with a perfect crust, the melt-in-your-mouth oxtail gnocchi, and for dessert, the sinful selection of donuts.

Mildred's Temple Kitchen

85 Hanna Avenue; tel: 416-588-5695; www.templekitchen.com; B Sat–Sun, daily L, D Thu–Sat; $$
A go-to spot for brunch on the weekends, this spacious and modern eatery is known city-wide for its stack of fluffy and thick blueberry-infused buttermilk pancakes. Not to miss either are the Huevos Monty with refried beans and

The bar at Rhum Corner   *A Cuban burger at La Cubana*

spicy salsa or the big brunch skillet with pulled pork and potato hash.

Miss Thing's

1279 Queen Street West; tel: 416-516-8677; www.missthings.com; D Tue–Sat; $$
Hawaiian cocktail and snack bar with a beautiful, sophisticated tropical decor to match. The drinks are top-notch and fun. For food, try the pineapple jicama salad and the poke bowl.

Nuit Social

1168 Queen Street West; tel: 647-350-6848; www.nuitsocial.com; daily D; $$
A late night favorite for the bar crowd, or anyone up for a delicious nibble or two, this cosy hangout specializes in charcuterie boards. Build your own board from a list of locally sourced and fine imported meats, cheeses, and olives, or pick from an Italian-inspired tapas menu.

Pho Tien Thanh

57 Ossington Avenue; tel: 416-588-6997; no website; daily L and D; $
Hole-in-the-wall Vietnamese restaurant to which locals flock for steaming hot bowls of pho – a classic Vietnamese soup consisting of a fragrant beef broth, rice noodles, fresh herbs, and thinly sliced meat.

Pinky's Ca Phe

53 Clinton Street; no phone, no website; Mon–Sat D; $$
Tucked away Vietnamese snack bar with an unassuming exterior, but the intimate and richly vintage decorated interior gives it an inviting and memorable atmosphere. Have a Foco Loco fruity cocktail with the full-flavored tiger's milk ceviche, the marrow beef, and the lemongrass chicken banh mi sandwich.

Pizzeria Libretto

221 Ossington Avenue; tel: 416-532-8000; www.pizzerialibretto.com; daily L and D; $$
Possibly the best, most authentic Neapolitan-style pizza in town, with several Toronto locations. Their savory pies are made with imported Italian ingredients and wood-fired in an oven made from imported Italian stones. The weekday lunch prix fixe deal is pretty good at $16 and includes a salad, pizza, and dessert.

Poutini's House of Poutine

1112 Queen Street West; tel: 647-342-3732; www.poutini.com; daily L and D; $
Poutine is a Canadian classic comfort dish and Poutini's does it really well. Hand-cut, twice-fried skin-on potato fries are topped with fresh local cheese curds and thick, 8-hour traditional gravy. Vegan cheese and vegetarian gravy are also available.

Rhum Corner

926 Dundas Street West; tel: 647-346-9356; www.rhumcorner.com; daily D; $$
Haitian watering hole, with simple, inexpensive, and also extremely tasty food and drinks. Go for the Pina Colada Slushie or Fresco cocktail, and share a

Seafood platter at the Tide and Vine Oyster House

few small plates of banana frites, salt cod patties, and albacore tuna ceviche.

Simit & Chai Co.

787 King Street West; tel: 647-352-4161; www.simitandchai.co; daily B and L; $
Spacious, industrial yet cosy Turkish bakery specializing in simit, circular breads filled with savory spreads like black olive paste or fava bean paste. Try them with Turkish coffee or tea.

Snakes & Lattes

600 Bloor Street West; tel: 647-342-9229; www.snakesandlattes.com; daily L and D; $
Pick a board game out of a collection of over 1,500, order some sandwiches and drinks, and get playing with your friends, or make new ones here at this concept café. The friendly staff can easily suggest a game and explain rules for any games that are unfamiliar.

Waterfront & Toronto Islands

Buster's Sea Cove

93 Front Street East (Upper Level of St Lawrence Market); tel: 416-369-9048; www.busters-seacove.com; Tue–Sat B and L; $
One of the busiest stands at the St Lawrence Market, Buster's is all about fresh and local seafood. Choose from traditional fish & chips or go for the crab cake sandwich, but expect a line-up and there are only a few spots to sit down.

Churrasco's

93 Front Street East (Upper Level of St Lawrence Market); tel: 416-862-2867;

www.stlawrencemarket.com; Tue–Sat B and L; $
Come here for the juiciest, most flavorful and tender rotisserie chicken basted in Churrasco's secret hot sauce. For dessert try their traditional Portuguese custard tarts – a sweet creamy egg custard filling inside a little, flaky pastry bowl.

Cruda Café

93 Front Street East (Upper Level of St Lawrence Market); tel: 647-346-6502; www.crudacafe.com; Tue–Sat B and L; $
Vegan eatery dedicated to using fresh, organic, and local ingredients to create dishes of living foods, either raw or cooked at low temperatures to ensure that all the nutrients remain intact.

European Delight

93 Front Street East (Lower Level of St Lawrence Market); tel: 416-365-9010; www.stlawrencemarket.com; Tue–Sat B and L; $
The specialty here is homemade Eastern European foods, such as Ukrainian pierogis, Hungarian blintzes, and Polish cabbage rolls, plus borscht, latkes, and other delicious take-out options.

Outside of Toronto

AG

5195 Magdalen Avenue, Niagara Falls; tel: 289-292-0005; www.agcuisine.com; Tue–Sun D; $$$
In amongst the neon lights and kitschy motels is this gem of a farm-to-table

Delectable Glory Hole Doughnuts

fine-dining establishment, located in the lower level of the Sterling Inn & Spa (see page 91). Much of the ingredients are grown on AG's own farm nearby, and all the wines are local. Try the grilled quail with a blueberry barley risotto, or the beef tenderloin with an almond brie crust.

Flour Mill Restaurant

6080 Fallsview Boulevard, Niagara Falls; tel: 905-357-1234; www.oldstoneinnhotel.com; B, L, and D daily; $$$

Inside the Old Stone Inn, which dates back to 1904, is this elegant and cozy restaurant boasting antique furnishings, creatively plated meals, and excellent service. The menu offers locally sourced produce, seafood, meats, and cheeses. Your best bet here is brunch, featuring delicious eggs benedict, NY strip steak & eggs, as well as other classic options.

Il Sorriso Café & Pizzeria

5983 Clark Avenue, Niagara Falls; tel: 905-353-1989; no website; Thu–Sat L and D; $$

Welcoming family-run Italian pizza joint known for its stone-baked, thin-crust pizza with a huge choice of toppings to satisfy any palate. The generously filled calzones are just as tasty, and try the fun s'mores pizza for dessert.

Tide and Vine Oyster House

3491 Portage Road, Niagara Falls; tel: 905-356-5782; www.tideandvine.com; L and D daily; $$

Casual but outstanding seafood restaurant and wine bar tucked away in a strip mall. The friendly staff will recommend their specialties, which include fresh oysters, grilled lobster, and a seafood chowder loaded with clams, scallops, shrimp, and fish.

Sweet Treats

Forno Cultura

609 King Street West; tel: 416-603-8305; www.fornocultura.com; Tue–Sat 7.30am–9.30pm, Sun 8am–6pm; $

Wonderful Italian bakery in an industrial space, offering sweet and savory breads, gorgeous mini-cakes, and addictive cookies, all using organic flour and natural ingredients.

Glory Hole Doughnuts

1596 Queen Street West; tel: 647-352-4848; www.gloryholedoughnuts.com; Mon–Fri 9am–6pm, Sat–Sun 10am–5pm; $

Inventive, freshly baked donuts are served here, with flavors such as banana cream pie, raspberry peach crumble, and peanut butter crunch.

Greg's Ice Cream

750 Spadina Avenue; tel: 416-962-4734; www.gregsicecream.com; daily 11.30am–11pm; $

Serving homemade, natural, and creamy ice cream since 1981 in a list of over 100 flavors. The best is the roasted marshmallow ice cream, though the coffee toffee is also delicious.

Outdoor tables at Bellwoods Brewery

NIGHTLIFE

Day or night, Toronto is pulsing with live music acts, swanky lounges, top dance clubs, and world-renowned theater productions. Enjoy a cozy cocktail in one of Little Italy's many late night eateries, check out the Ossington Strip or Queen Street West for vibrant cafés and bars, head into a busy pub in The Annex, or seek out the hottest nightclubs in the Entertainment District.

From intimate venues to spaces that can entertain thousands, you won't have trouble finding local and international musicians performing. And for hilarious comedy shows, there are stand-up acts happening all across the city.

Bars

Bar + Karaoke Lounge

360 Yonge Street; tel: 416-340-7154; www.bar-plus.com

While not in Koreatown, this is one of the city's best karaoke bars. It features private, stylish, and well-kept rooms, good service, and lots of songs to choose from.

BarChef

472 Queen Street West; tel: 416-868-4800; www.barcheftoronto.com

For a cocktail lounge, Gothic-like BarChef is the best, featuring the top mixologists in the city, who are always busy creating amazing drinks accompanied by an easy-going soundtrack. Try the bay leaf and elderflower spritz or the vanilla hickory smoked Manhattan.

Bellwoods Brewery

124 Ossington Avenue; tel: 416-535-4586; www.bellwoodsbrewery.com

Bright and industrial, this brewpub has a comfortable cottage-like decor. There's an excellent selection of house-brewed beer and accompanying bites to eat. The outdoor patio out front is one of the best spots for a drink when the weather is cooperating.

Birreria Volo

612 College Street; tel: 416-498-5786; www.birreriavolo.com

Here you walk into an exposed-brick alleyway with a ceiling, find a spot at the narrow bar, the communal seating at the back, or the summer patio, and pick one of the 26 craft beers on tap. This is Little Italy's, if not the city's, coolest, industrial beer bar. Light bar snacks are available as well.

The Boat

158 Augusta Avenue; tel: 416-593-9218; www.theboatkensington.com

Always attracting local crowds, this nautical-themed, casual bar in the heart of Kensington Market often hosts live music. Drinks are inexpensive and plentiful, the dance floor is spacious, and the range of music will suit most tastes.

Hair-raising Drake Underground

The Caledonian

856 College Street; tel: 416-577-7472;
www.thecaledonian.ca

An inviting Scottish pub in Little Italy that boasts a huge whisky menu of over 300 malts and blends, plus special Scottish beers on tap. Of course, haggis is on the menu, as are Scotch eggs, fish and chips, and meat pies.

CC Lounge & Whisky Bar

45 Front Street East; tel: 416-362-4777;
www.cconfront.com

For whisky lovers, this historical restaurant and bar, with a 1920s prohibition era decor, specializes in whiskies – over 300 of them. You can also tour the onsite tunnel, built in 1891, which was used to facilitate the illegal trade and smuggling of prohibited spirits.

The Dakota Tavern

249 Ossington Avenue; tel: 416-850-4579;
www.thedakotatavern.com

Long-standing local favorite dive bar, located in a basement, with a country vibe and nightly live music acts. Standard beers and well drinks, and on the weekends the Bluegrass Brunch features a live band accompanied by a satisfying breakfast menu.

Drake Underground

1150 Queen Street West; tel: 416-531-5042; www.thedrake.ca

One of the top bars and music venues in the city, The Drake Hotel's subterranean space is constantly hopping with DJs, live indie music, movie screenings, and comedy performances. You can also head upstairs to the lounge or rooftop patio of the hotel for a drink or bite to eat.

The Emmet Ray

924 College Street; tel: 416-792-4497;
www.theemmetray.com

An inviting, classy bar with an extensive whisky list, elevated pub fare, and nightly entertainment, including live music and stand-up comedy nights.

The Gaslight

1426 Bloor Street West; tel: 647-402-9728;
www.thegaslightto.com

A warm and friendly candle-lit watering hole with church pews for seating and music just quiet enough to allow for good conversation. The drinks menu includes local wines, craft beers, and simple cocktails. A modest snack menu of comfort foods such as charcuterie boards and pizzas is on offer as well.

Handlebar

159 August Avenue; tel: 647-748-7433;
www.thehandlebar.ca

For a local beer or simple whisky, plus homey and budget-friendly snacks, this intimate neighborhood bar in Kensington Market has a lively karaoke night on Tuesdays, plus DJs spin retro tunes on weekends. Up-and-coming live music acts frequent the place as well.

Horseshoe Tavern

370 Queen Street West; tel: 416-598-4226;

Serving up at The Lockhart

www.horseshoetavern.com

Legendary bar and music venue, dating back to the 1950s. Once upon a time big names, including Willie Nelson, the Talking Heads, and the Rolling Stones, played here. Excellent live performances continue to this day, and the A&W take-out window is just plain fun.

King Taps

100 King Street West; tel: 647-361-2025; www.kingtaps.com

With over 50 beers on tap, this sprawling, two-story sports bar has an extensive pub food menu as well. The outdoor patios are packed during lunchtime, and there are big-screen TVs all over the place so you won't miss a game. Try the beer flights for a good selection, along with a wood-fired pizza.

The Lockhart

1479 Dundas Street West; tel: 647-748-4434; www.thelockhart.ca

An unofficial and subtle Harry Potter-themed bar in the Little Portugal neighborhood with excellent and inventive cocktails, local craft beers, and a creative tapas menu. Brunch is available on weekends.

Mahjong Bar

1276 Dundas Street West; tel: 647-980-5664; www.mahjongbar.com

Hidden behind a small, pink-painted convenience store, this stylish retro bar, with its soft red glow, serves fresh tropical cocktails, unusual beers, and delicate Chinese appetizers. Try the Green Dragon cocktail, made with gin, melon, lemon, and egg white, alongside the Mahjong Half Moon meat and vegetable pockets.

Mulberry Bar

828 Bloor Street West; no phone; www.mulberry.bar

Elegant, light-and-lush, plant-filled Parisian cocktail bar with a pretty, street-side seasonal patio. The cocktails created here are dreamy and sophisticated, and the wines pair well with the imported French cheeses.

Pray Tell

838 College Street; tel: 647-340-7729; www.praytellbar.com

Gorgeous Scandinavian-inspired bar-café that locals pop into any time of day, for brunch, an after work drink, or for late night cocktails and tapas. The gourmet Asian-fusion food menu offers delicious seafood options, pork belly dumplings, and tender short ribs.

The Shameful Tiki Room

1378 Queen Street West; no phone; www.shamefultikiroom.com

Decked out in bamboo and wicker, the low-lit, Polynesian atmosphere here is perfect for a fancy tropical cocktail or two. Try the Mystery Bowl drink, ideally for two or more people. The kitchen makes delicious snacks until the wee hours, including mini burger sliders, fish tacos, deep fried crab wontons, and chicken satay.

Retro Tennessee   *Cocktail time at The Shameful Tiki Room*

Tennessee

1554 Queen Street West; tel: 416-535-7777; www.tennesseetavern.ca

Kitschy, historic bar with unique vintage decor and an Eastern European food and drink menu. The stage is frequently filled with live music acts, and there's a comfortable back patio. With your imported beer, go for the freshly baked pretzels, the schnitzels, and they even have trout caviar.

Three Speed

1163 Bloor Street West; tel: 647-430-3834; no website

Friendly neighborhood pub where the backyard-feel patio is the main attraction. It features an old fireplace, lush plants, and plenty of locals. Come for a simple but satisfying brunch on weekends, or stay late for beers and sandwiches.

Track & Field Bar

860 College Street; no phone; www.trackandfieldbar.com

A vast, subterranean bar devoted to indoor lawn games. Half of the bocce ball courts and shuffleboards are free to use and are first come first serve. The other half can be reserved for a fee. Patrons are also welcome to bring in their own food as the bar only has fries on the menu.

Movie Theaters

For a list of all movie theaters in Toronto, check out cinemaclock.com/ont/toronto/theatres. And for an unforgetta-ble movie experience, head to the Cinesphere Imax theater at Ontario Science Centre (see page 76).

Carlton Cinema

20 Carlton Street; tel: 416-598-5454; www.imaginecinemas.com

Old-school movie theater from the early 80s, still going strong. It shows new Hollywood releases, second-run movies, plus independent and foreign movies. Tuesdays tickets are just $5.

The Fox Theatre

2236 Queen Street East; tel: 416-691-7335; www.foxtheatre.ca

Dating back to 1914, this vintage and restored, Beaches neighborhood, single-screen movie theater plays a mixture of second-run, independent and foreign movies, plus special event screenings. It's also licensed so you can have a drink with your popcorn.

Varsity Cinemas

55 Bloor Street; tel: 416-961-6304; www.cineplex.com

All the big blockbusters will be playing at this modern, multiplex theater, so it's always buzzing with people. There's a VIP theater here as well, which is for adults only and allows for dinner and drinks to be served right to your comfortable seats.

Comedy Clubs

Comedy Bar

945 Bloor Street West; tel: 416-551-6540;

Roy Thomson Hall

www.comedybar.ca

Excellent, if sometimes off-beat, performers tell their best jokes in this modest space. Tickets are relatively inexpensive here as new and upcoming talents are frequently on stage.

The Second City Theatre

51 Mercer Street; tel: 416-343-0011; www.secondcity.com

The starting point for many famous comedians and award-winning actors, this premier comedy club has live sketch and improv shows every night. Shows combine comedy with entertaining theatrics, dance, and music, and often includes the participation of the audience as well. They also have a second, more intimate location – the John Candy Box Theatre at 99 Blue Jays Way; tel: 416-340-7270.

Nightclubs

Coda

794 Bathurst Street; tel: 416-536-0346; www.codatoronto.com

EDM (electronic dance music) enthusiasts flock to this sprawling, two-story club near Koreatown, where DJs pump up the volume on the weekends and club-goers relish in the deep sounds and flashing lights.

Wildflower

550 Wellington Street West; tel: 647-778-8462; www.loveusnot.com

Located downstairs, inside the prestigious Thompson Hotel, this sleek, modern lounge resembles a vast art gallery. DJs play all the top hits and its clientele are well dressed. The Thompson Hotel also has a chic rooftop lounge and pool for cocktails and sushi.

Jazz and Blues Bars

Poetry Jazz Café

Lively, casual, dimly-lit bar hidden behind graffiti-clad wooden sliding doors in the Kensington Market neighborhood. Nightly live performances include experimental jazz, soul, funk, and blues. Cocktails here are excellent as well, notably the Bitches Brew concocted with aged dark Caribbean rum, tequila, grapefruit, brown sugar, lime, and spices.

The Reservoir Lounge

52 Wellington Street East; tel: 416-955-0887; www.reservoirlounge.com

Five nights a week a different band is playing a different sound, with a general jazz and blues theme, at this busy and intimate live music and dance lounge. And if you're hungry, they make good pizzas too.

The Rex Hotel Jazz and Blues Bar

194 Queen Street West; tel: 416-598-2475; www.therex.ca

Since the early 1980s, The Rex has been part of the city's thriving local jazz scene. Every night there's an excellent band on stage here, from local talent to world-renowned musicians from across the globe.

Koerner Hall

Theaters and Performing Arts

See also the Entertainment section. For the Elgin Theater, see page 32.

Ed Mirvish Theatre

244 Victoria Street; tel: 416-872-1212 (TicketKing); www.mirvish.com
First built in 1920, this historic and elegant film and play theatre shows big Broadway and London musicals. Guided tours can be arranged to take a closer look at the carefully restored and lavish interior.

Four Seasons Centre for the Performing Arts

145 Queen Street West; tel: 416-363-8231 (Box Office); www.coc.ca
Home to the Canadian Opera Company and the National Ballet of Canada, this modern building was purpose built for opera and ballet and features the finest level of acoustics. Note that you can get rush tickets and standing room tickets that go on sale at 11am on the day of the performances. These are discounted tickets and are limited.

Koerner Hall

273 Bloor Street West; tel: 416-408-0208; www.rcmusic.com
One of North America's most acoustically superb concert halls, and where The Royal Conservatory presents the best of jazz, opera, pop, classical, and world music performers.

Roy Thomson Hall

60 Simcoe Street; tel: 416-872-4255 (box office); www.roythomsonhall.com
Designed by Canadian architect Arthur Erickson, this modernist circular building built in the early 1980s is home to the Toronto Symphony Orchestra and the Toronto Mendelssohn Choir. It is also one of the main venues for the Toronto International Film Festival (TIFF).

Free Concerts

The Free Concert Series at the Four Seasons Centre for the Performing Arts starts in late September and runs until May, taking place most Tuesdays and Thursdays at noon, and some Wednesdays at noon or 5.30pm. Artists from around the world share their talents in vocals, piano, jazz, dance, chamber, and world music. Admission is on a first-come, first-served basis and seating is limited.

Centreville Amusement Park, on Centre Island

A–Z

A

Age Restrictions

The legal drinking age is 19 in the province of Ontario, while the legal driving age is 16, with restrictions.

B

Budgeting

Average costs

A beer or glass of house wine: $7

A main course (budget $10, moderate $15, and expensive $30)

Accommodations (budget under $100, moderate $150–400, and expensive over $400)

A taxi journey to/from the main airport to Downtown Toronto: $50–70

A single bus ticket, subway ticket, street car ticket: $3.25

The CityPASS Toronto pass includes admission to the CN Tower, Casa Loma, Royal Ontario Museum, Ripley's Aquarium of Canada, and the Toronto Zoo or Ontario Science Centre. It also has the benefit of allowing pass holders to skip most ticket lines. CityPASS can be purchased online (www.citypass.com/toronto) or at the participating attractions, and cost approximately $100 for adults and $70 for kids, offering a savings of 38 percent if all attractions are visited.

C

Children

Toronto is a very family friendly city. Many hotels have excellent packages that often allow children under a certain age to stay free of charge, plus they'll have babysitting services and cribs available. Most restaurants will produce children's menus and perhaps even a supply of paper and crayons to keep them occupied. Shopping malls and parks frequently have children's play areas. Restaurants and movie theaters will also provide booster seats for smaller children. Attractions usually always have discounts for children, depending on their age.

Clothing

Wear layers no matter what time of year you are visiting Toronto, with an added extra warm coat and boots for winter time, and a light waterproof jacket, plus comfortable walking shoes.

Crime and Safety

Toronto is one of the safest cities in North America. However, it is still a large city and visitors should always use common sense when walking around after dark and in unfamiliar areas.

Anyone in an emergency situation should phone 911, and the call will be forwarded to police, fire department, or

Police cars

ambulance, depending upon the reason for the call.

In case your documentation is stolen, it's a good idea to have two photocopies of your passport identification page, airline tickets, driver's license, and the credit cards that you plan to bring with you. Leave one photocopy of this with family or friends at home; pack the other in a place separate from where you carry your valuables.

Pickpockets are not unheard of, especially in crowded places like a busy subway station, but it is not a huge problem in Toronto, and simply requires being mindful of how you carry your wallet or any other valuables.

Customs Regulations

Canada's customs requirements for vacation visitors are fairly simple. Personal effects for use during the stay may be brought into the country. There is no problem with bringing rental cars from the US, but drivers should always carry a copy of the contract with them in the car (this is also important if stopped by police for any reason).

Limits on duty-free tobacco, alcohol, and personal gifts are similar to other countries, but perhaps a bit stricter. For more details on Customs regulations and what you can bring to Canada, contact: Canada Border Services Agency, tel: 204-983-3500 or 506-636 5064 from outside Canada and 1-800-461-9999 from inside Canada; www.cbsa-asfc.gc.ca.

Pets require a veterinary's certificate of good health and vaccinations. Many foods and plants are prohibited, so check the rules before arriving. The rules for a food type may be different depending whether you are coming from the United States or from another country. The Canada Border Services Agency website has full details: www.cbsa-asfc.gc.ca.

Citizens of the UK may bring home, duty-free: 200 cigarettes or 50 cigars; 2 liters of wine OR 1 liter of liquor; and additional goods totaling no more than £390 ($675).

Each American citizen who spends more than 48 hours in Canada may return with $800 worth of goods, duty-free. Some airports and border points feature duty-free stores, offering liquor and other goodies, but make sure you know your prices before jumping at the 'bargains'. And remember that tax is not included in the displayed price. Americans should direct their questions to any US Customs Office or visit its website at www.cbp.gov, while travelers from other countries should contact the Customs Office in their own country for information on what they can bring back.

Disabled Travelers

The Canadian Transportation Agency offers an online guide for disabled visitors traveling by air in Canada, which

The Toronto Light Festival in the Distillery District

can be accessed at www.otc-cta.gc.ca. Another useful online source for people with disabilities is the Government of Canada's www.travel.gc.ca/travelling/health-safety/disabilities.

Airlines, buses, and trains all offer wheelchair assistance, although you should allow extra time before commencing your journey. Taking a wheelchair on the train requires advanced notice, so it is recommended to call VIA Rail 48 hours beforehand (toll free tel: 1-888-842-7245, www.viarail.ca).

Access, especially for those in wheelchairs, can be found in almost every public building across the city, and most museums, tourist information centers, and visitor attractions have taken steps to make access easier. Hotels, especially those affiliated with chains, generally provide disabled accommodations and restroom facilities. Many national and provincial parks offer alternative trails that are accessible to disabled travelers.

Designated spaces for disabled drivers are generally available at parking lots in cities, at shopping malls, and in the parking lots of large stores. Official parking permits issued from countries within the European Union and the US can be used in Canada. Visitors from elsewhere in the world may also use their parking permits in Canada; however, as there are no official agreements with other countries, it is recommended to carry a copy of your official documentation from your issuing agency.

E

Electricity

Canada operates on 110 volts in common with the US. Sockets accommodate plugs with two flat or two flat and one round pins, so an adapter is required for the use of European appliances.

Embassies and Consulates

While foreign visitors are traveling in and across Canada, they may need to contact their own country in case of an emergency. Consulates can be most helpful, for example, if a passport is stolen or if a message needs to be relayed quickly back home. The following list gives details of all the consulates located in Toronto.

Australia 175 Bloor Street E, Ste 1100, tel: 416-323-4280

France 2 Bloor Street E, Ste 2200, tel: 416-847-1900

Ireland 1 First Canadian Place, Ste 2650, tel: 416-366-9300

UK College Park, 777 Bay Street, Ste 2800, tel: 416-593-1290

US 360 University Avenue, tel: 416-595-1700

Emergencies

Visitors are urged to obtain travel medical insurance before leaving their own country. Anyone using prescription medicine should bring an adequate supply, as well as a copy of the prescription in

Caribbean Carnival dancers

case it needs to be renewed. Travelers requiring medical attention needn't worry – hospitals in Toronto are known for their high medical standards.

In an emergency requiring the police, an ambulance or fire truck, immediate help can be summoned by dialing 911. Emergency telephone numbers are listed in the front of all local telephone directories. If caught in a legal bind, foreign visitors should contact their consulates, a partial listing of which is shown in the Embassies and Consulates section.

Etiquette

Good manners are valued: hold doors open for people following you; don't jump the line; let people get off public transportation before you get on; offer your seat to older passengers or pregnant women; on escalators, stand on the right, walk past on the left.

F

Festivals

Mid-January to early March
The Toronto Light Festival. The Distillery Historic District is lit up all winter long with light installations by local and international artists.

Early February
Winterlicious. More than 200 restaurants participate in this food festival, offering a series of culinary events across the city.

March
Toronto Comicon. Comic book and pop culture convention featuring high-profile guests, presentations, and workshops.

Late April to early May
Hot Docs International Documentary Festival. The largest documentary festival in North America, screening films from around the globe, plus forums and award ceremonies.

May
Doors Open Toronto. Each year in May, for one weekend only, buildings across the city of architectural, historical, cultural, and social significance not usually open to the public open their doors to visitors.

June
North by Northeast. Music and arts festival with live performances, media displays, gaming, and interactive conferences. www.nxne.com

Luminato. A magnificent 10-day international festival of arts and creativity, held at indoor and outdoor locations citywide. www.luminato.com

Pride Month. One of the largest Prides in the world, with a celebration of Canada's inclusiveness, including an arts and cultural program. www.pridetoronto.com

TD Toronto Jazz Festival. The world's greatest jazz musicians come to perform in the city's best music venues. www.torontojazz.com

Santa Claus Parade marching band

July

Canada Day. Countrywide celebrations with concerts, street entertainment, and fireworks. www.toronto.ca

Beaches International Jazz Festival. Free 10-day music festival in the lakeside Beaches community with an excellent line-up of food trucks. www.beachesjazz.com

Toronto Fringe Festival. Toronto's largest theater festival, with over 150 international theater companies performing all over the city. www.fringetoronto.com

Toronto Caribbean Carnival. The city's West Indian community celebrates with singing, dancing, and parades, mostly on the Toronto Islands, creating a Mardi Gras atmosphere. www.torontocaribbeancarnival.com

August

Canadian National Exhibition. The largest and oldest exhibition of its kind in the world, featuring air shows, big-name entertainment, and all sorts of exhibits. All this takes place for three weeks at Exhibition Place on Lake Shore Boulevard. www.theex.com

September

Toronto International Film Festival. A 10-day showcase of the best in global moviemaking. www.tiff.net

Nuit Blanche. An extraordinary celebration of contemporary art, in galleries, museums, and countless unexpected places from sunset to sunrise. www.scotiabanknuitblanche.ca

November

Santa Claus Parade. A Toronto tradition since 1913, watch a parade of fantastic floats, marching bands, dancers pass by along with thousands of eager spectators. www.thesantaclausparade.com

Ice-skating performance during the Canadian National Exhibition

Bright eyes at the Christmas market

December

The Toronto Christmas Market. Month-long event featuring a traditional Christmas market, European-style, in the Distillery Historic District. www.torontochristmasmarket.com

Health

As foreign visitors to Toronto are not eligible for healthcare it is important to be covered by health insurance for the duration of your trip. It may also be advisable to ensure coverage for emergency evacuation with a medical escort to your country of residence. Some Canadian companies offer "Visitors to Canada" travel medical insurance that can be purchased online.

If you are entering Canada with prescription drugs and syringes used for medical reasons, be sure to keep the medication in its original and labeled container to avoid problems. Syringes should be accompanied by a medical certificate that shows they are for medical use and should be declared to Canadian Customs officials. You should carry with you an extra prescription from your doctor in the event your medication is lost or stolen and to attest to your need to take such prescriptions.

Pharmacies and Hospitals

Pharmacies can be found throughout the city and can provide basic home health care supplies and advice.

Shoppers Drug Mart, 2345 Yonge Street, 416-487-5411, open 24hrs.
Mount Sinai Hospital, 600 University Avenue, 416-596-4200
St Michael's Hospital, 30 Bond Street, 416-360-4000

Hours and Holidays

Standard business hours for stores are 10am–6pm. Drug and convenience stores generally close at 11pm, but some operate for 24 hours. Banking hours vary greatly; the majority of banks now open long hours, which may include Saturdays, and also, in some instances, Sundays. ATMs (bank machines) are readily available.

Banks, schools, government offices, and many beer and liquor stores close on national holidays. Hotels, restaurants, and most retail outlets stay open. Most museums and art galleries offer extended hours on one or more nights a week, and sometimes admission is free at certain times.

Statutory Holidays

January 1 New Year's Day
July 1 Canada Day
November 11 Remembrance Day
December 25 Christmas Day
December 26 Boxing Day
Movable Statutory Holidays:
Ontario Family Day (3rd Monday in February)
Good Friday
Monday preceding May 24 (Victoria Day, the Queen's birthday)

The choice is yours

Civic Holiday (1st Monday in August)
Labour Day (1st Monday in September)
Thanksgiving Day (2nd Monday in October)

I

Internet

Numerous coffee shops, restaurants, and bars routinely offer free Wifi access; or you can visit any public library. Note that usually there is a time limit for usage of a library's computer. Most hotels and airports have free room internet access or business centers where you can access emails and the internet.

L

Language

English and French are the official languages of Canada, though English is more widely spoken outside of the province of Quebec, where French is more dominant.

LGBTQ Travelers

Toronto became the first city in North America to legalize same-sex marriage in 2003, and the city's Pride festival is one of the largest in the world. Church and Wellesley streets are the hub of Toronto's LGBTQ community, and the neighborhoods of Leslieville, Cabbagetown, Queen West, the Annex, and Kensington have plenty of LGBTQ-friendly cafés and bars. Check the *Daily Xtra* (www.dailyxtra.com) for the latest news and events in the Village. The 519, at 519 Church Street (tel: 416-392-6874, www.the519.org), is also a great resource for events, services, and support.

M

Media

Newspapers and Magazines

The National Post, *The Globe and Mail*, the *Toronto Star*, and the *Toronto Sun* are Toronto's major newspapers. *NOW Toronto* is an alternative free weekly paper, and *Toronto Life*, *Where Toronto*, and *The Walrus* are all excellent Toronto-focused monthly magazines. Newsstands sell major American, British, and French newspapers and magazines.

Radio and Television

The Canadian Broadcasting Company (CBC) operates two nationwide television networks (English and French), along with an all-news network. CTV Global broadcasts two others. Regional and provincial networks, along with independent and US broadcasters, account for the rest.

Cable networks enable viewers to see programs produced in all parts of Canada and the US, along with a sampling of programs from the UK, Australia, France, and other countries. CBC operates a national radio network, both AM and FM, in English and French. There are hundreds of private stations that fill the airwaves with news and music.

The Cathedral Church of St James

Money

Currency

The currency in Toronto is the Canadian dollar ($). Canadian and US dollars have a different rate of exchange. All dollar prices quoted in this book are in Canadian dollars.

Visitors may bring up to $10,000 into Canada without reporting it. When exchanging money, you may be required to provide your passport or other identification. Canadian banks and foreign exchange bureaus will convert funds, often at very attractive rates. US funds are readily accepted by many department stores and hotels, etc, but they may not offer the most advantageous rate.

Credit Cards

Major credit cards are widely accepted in Toronto's cafés, restaurants, stores, attractions, and hotels. Car rental companies will require a credit card.

Cash Machines

ATMs are available throughout the city as well as inside convenience stores and bars.

Traveler's Checks

Traveler's checks are not widely used in Canada anymore, as debit and credit cards are preferred. If you do buy traveler's checks, ask your bank about overseas charges and make sure to buy them denominated in Canadian dollars. American Express, Thomas Cook, and Visa traveler's checks are still accepted, but generally at banks rather than retailers.

Tipping and Taxes

A 15–20 percent tip is expected for good service at a restaurant, while a 5 percent tip is sufficient for taxi drivers. A 13 percent sales tax is added on to most goods and services (be careful, it is not included in the displayed price), plus an additional 4 percent tax for accommodations, and some restaurants will automatically add a service tip for large groups.

P

Postal Services

Canada Post and international courier companies provide express services across the country and to foreign destinations. Canada Post locations are listed in the business section of the telephone directory. Mail boxes are typically red. Stamps are readily available at post offices (open Mon–Fri during business hours) and local convenience and drug stores.

Costs. At the time of writing, postcard to Europe ($2.50), letter to Europe ($3.60), postcard to the US ($1.20), letter to the US ($1.80).

Main Post Office. Toronto has dozens of post offices, but the oldest, and still operating one, dating from 1834, is located at 260 Adelaide Street East. It also houses a neat little museum.

Bikes for hire

R

Religion

Roman Catholics are the largest religious group in Toronto, with Protestants in second place. Muslims, Sikhs, Hindus, Buddhists, and Jews are also represented. Any hotel concierge will direct you to the nearest place of worship. Religious tolerance is noted by the harmonic blend of Toronto's multicultural population.

S

Smoking

If you are a smoker, you'll have to look carefully to find a place to light up, as smoking is banned in most public places and it is forbidden to smoke within 9 meters (30ft) of the entrance of a public building. Vapers beware too, there is also legislation in the pipeline to ban vaping in the same places where smoking is banned. All hotel rooms are non-smoking, too.

T

Telephones

The telephone system in Canada is similar to that in the US. Payphone costs begin at 50 cents, but they can be hard to find in the city. For collect or other operator-assisted calls, dial "0" then the number you wish to reach. Dial "1" (Canada's country code), then the area code for Toronto (416 or 647), and then the seven subsequent numbers for long-distance calls charged to the originating phone.

International Dialing Codes
Australia +61
Ireland +353
UK +44
US +1

Cell Phones

If your cell phone service provider uses the world-standard GSM network, you should be able to use your phone in Toronto, but watch out for those steep roaming fees. Consider purchasing a new SIM card to use for the duration of your visit in Toronto. Rogers, Bell, Telus, Fido, and Virgin are the major cell phone companies in the city. Phones can be rented as well from various cell phone shops.

Time Zones

Toronto is in the Eastern Standard Time zone, which is 5 hours behind GMT. For example, when it's noon in London, it is 7am in Toronto. Daylight saving time begins the second Sunday in March and ends the first Sunday in November.

Tourist Information

Pick up maps, visitor guides, and brochures from the Toronto Tourist Information Centre at 65 Front Street West, 416-392-9300, www.seetorontonow.com. It's open seven days a week, 10am–6pm.

Streetcar in Downtown

Tours and Guides

City Sightseeing Toronto (249 Queens Quay West; tel: 416-410-0536; www. citysightseeingtoronto.com). Offers hop-on-hop-off double decker bus tours around the city, plus day tours to Niagara Falls.

Distillery District Segway Tours (30 Gristmill Lane; tel: 416-642-0008; www.gotourscanada.com). Segways are a two-wheeled personal transportation vehicle and this tour company can first train you on the Segway and then take you through the Distillery Historic District on various tours, including a ghost tour and a winter tour.

Toronto Bicycle Tours (275 Dundas Street West; tel: 416-477-2184; www. torontobicycletours.com). Bicycle tours explore Downtown, the Toronto Islands, and beyond. Tours include a bicycle, helmet, water, and snacks.

Toronto Harbour Tours (145 Queens Quay West; tel: 416-203-6994; www. harbourtourstoronto.ca). Offers boat tours around the harbour and around the Toronto Islands. Chartered water taxis to the Toronto Islands can also be arranged, which is especially handy when the ferries are full in summer.

Transportation

Arrival by Air

Most Canadian and international airlines arrive at Canada's busiest and largest airport, Toronto Pearson International Airport (YYZ). Some domestic airlines fly in and out of the smaller Billy Bishop Toronto City Airport (YTZ), located on an island just off the lakeshore.

YYZ is located 23km (14 miles) northwest of Downtown and has two main terminals, number 1 and number 3. The UP Express train is the best and fastest way to get downtown from the airport, and there are also buses, taxis, and car rental companies onsite.

Public Transportation

Bus

Toronto Transit Commission (TTC) has a network of over 150 bus routes throughout the city, connecting to the airports and subway stations. The TTC also has a streetcar system with eleven routes concentrated Downtown. Tickets for buses, streetcars, and the subway cost $3.25 for a single adult fare, and a day pass costs $12.50.

Subway

The subway system in Toronto has two main lines, the 1 Yonge-University line and the 2 Bloor-Danforth line, both connecting the downtown core with the surrounding neighborhoods. These lines eventually connect to line 3 Scarborough and line 4 Sheppard.

Rail

GO Transit operates a commuter rail and bus service, connecting the city to the rest of the Greater Toronto Area. The Union Pearson Express rail link service takes you from the airport to downtown under 25minutes and costs $24. Amtrak has service from Chicago and

Ferry to the islands

New York to Toronto, and VIA Rail connects Toronto to most of the other major Canadian cities.

Ferries

The Toronto Islands in Lake Ontario are accessed via the Toronto Island Ferries, of which there are three. They depart from the Jack Layton Ferry Terminal, which is located at the foot of Bay Street. The Billy Bishop Toronto City Airport is accessed this way as well, though via a separate ferry than those heading to the Toronto Islands, in addition to a pedestrian tunnel that connects the airport terminal to the mainland at Eireann Quay.

Taxis

Airport taxis, located at the arrival levels at both terminals of the Toronto Pearson International Airport, cost about $60 to downtown Toronto and the trip takes approximately 30 minutes. City taxis can be hailed from the streets or you can call ahead. Average fares for a taxi ride across downtown will cost about $15 plus a tip of 5 percent. Ridesharing companies such as Uber and Lyft also operate in the city.

Beck Taxis 416-751-5555
City Taxis 416-740-2222
Diamond Taxis 416-366-6868
Royal Taxis 416-777-9222

Driving

High gas prices, congested streets, and parking hassles make driving a car in Toronto less than ideal. It is only recommended for those who wish to see many of the sites and attractions outside of the city, such as Niagara Falls, and the Niagara Wine Region.

A foreign driver's license is accepted for a stay of up to three months, after which an international driver's license is required. In Ontario, drivers must be at least 21 years of age to rent a car. All

Taxi in downtown Toronto

Female tourists in the Distillery District

major car rental companies have locations in Toronto and at the Toronto Pearson International Airport.

Budget 1-800-268-8900/905-676-1500

Enterprise 1-800-RENT-ACAR/416-798-1465

Hertz 1-800-263-0600/416-674-2020

National Car Rental 1-800-CAR-RENT/905-676-4000

Visas and Passports

All visitors to Canada who are not Canadian citizens or Canadian permanent residents must carry a valid passport with at least six months remaining before its expiration, including minors. An Electronic Travel Authorization (eTA) is required for visitors from visa-exempt countries, except for US citizens, and must be purchased prior to departure from their home country. It costs $7 and can be applied for online (www.canada.ca). Visitors from non-visa-waiver countries must apply for a visa prior to arriving in Canada.

Washrooms

Public washrooms are generally clean and always free to use in the city. They can be found in shopping malls, subway stations, parks, and visitor information offices. Some restaurants and cafés may allow you to use their washrooms even though you haven't made a purchase with them. Other options would be to hop inside a hotel, theater, or large grocery store and use their public washrooms.

Weights and Measures

Canada uses the metric system, but many things are still expressed in the imperial system and some people speak of "miles" and "pounds." For example, if you ask directions, someone may tell you how far away something is in miles or, if it is closer, in yards. In grocery stores, as often as not, you will see both the price per pound and the price per kilogram or per 100 grams.

1 centimeter (cm) = 0.394ins
1 kilometer (km) = 0.621 miles
1 liter = 0.22 UK gallon
1 liter = 0.26 US gallon (g)
1 kilogram = 2.2lbs

Women Travelers

Toronto is probably one of the safest cities in the world for women to travel alone. With so many women traveling on business, hotels and restaurants are fully accustomed to seeing women on their own and are becoming increasingly sensitive to their concerns. Provided a female traveler follows a common sense-based code of conduct, the chances of running into a problem should be minimal. A hotel's concierge can be a reliable source of information on suitable or safe places to go and acceptable routes to get there.

A selection at Indigo Bookstore

BOOKS AND FILM

Canada has a strong literary tradition, and Margaret Atwood, who is an Ottawa native but has lived in Toronto for most of her life, is arguably the country's best known author (*The Blind Assassin*, and *The Handmaid's Tale* for example – the latter of which is now a television series). Similarly, authors Michael Ignatieff (former politician and author of *Scar Tissue*), Cory Doctorow (*Down and Out in the Magic Kingdom*), Louise Penny (*Chief Inspector Armand Gamache* series), Mark Steyn (*America Alone: The End of the World As We Know It*), and Jane Urquhart (*The Whirlpool, The Stone Carvers*) all hail from the city.

Known as Hollywood North, alongside the city of Vancouver on the West Coast, Toronto's film and television industry is buzzing. The city is home to such series as *Designated Survivor, Suits, Star Trek: Discovery,* and many more. Director David Cronenberg (*Videodrome, eXistenZ, A History of Violence, Crash*) and comedian Howie Mandel (*Deal or No Deal*), both Torontonians, have helped shape both sides of the industry.

Fiction

The Blind Assassin by Margaret Atwood. A historical science fiction novel set in Toronto during the 1930s and 1940s.

Cat's Eye by Margaret Atwood. An emotional story about a controversial painter who reflects on her life growing up in Toronto.

The Robber Bride by Margaret Atwood. Set in Toronto during the 1990s, this grisly tale is inspired by the Brothers Grimm story but with a twist – an evil villainess lurking around in Toronto all but kills three of her old college acquaintances.

The Incomparable Atuk by Mordecai Richler. A satirical novel about a young Inuit man who moves to Toronto and learns to adapt to the ways of the big city.

In the Skin of a Lion by Michael Ondaatje. A mystery and love story about immigrant life set in Toronto during the 1920s and 1930s.

Consolation by Michael Redhill. Follows the story of two families in Toronto living centuries apart, with an unusual connection.

Headhunter by Timothy Findley. Set in a dystopic Toronto during a raging epidemic.

Cabbagetown by Hugh Garner. A young man faces the bleak prospects of the dirty thirties during the Depression in Toronto's Cabbagetown neighborhood.

Unless by Carol Shields. The final novel by Shields, this semi-autobiographical fictional story recalls the difficulties of a dysfunctional family living in Toronto.

Michelle Williams and Seth Rogan in Take This Waltz

Non-Fiction

No Mean City by Eric Arthur. A quintessential book on Toronto's architectural heritage and contemporary designs.

Toronto Between the Wars by Charles Cotter. Takes a hard look at the city between the period of WWI and WWII and includes 180 striking photographs. Toronto: Biography of a City by Allan Levine. Explores four centuries of the city's history and it's politics, ethnic diversity, and overall development.

Toronto Then and Now by Doug Taylor. Coffee-table-style book that examines 75 heritage sites throughout the city and illustrates the changes that have taken place during the last century.

Film

Strange Brew, 1983. In this famous comedy based on SCTV (Second City Television – a Canadian sketch comedy show) characters, local actors Rick Moranis and Dave Thomas, who also served as a co-directors, get involved in a brewery mystery, with most film shots based in Toronto and nearby surrounding areas.

Dead Ringers, 1988. Directed by David Cronenberg, this thriller was set and filmed throughout the city, including various scenes at Casa Loma and Trinity Square Park.

Exotica, 1994. Canadian film director Atom Egoyan's breakthrough drama about a fictional strip club set in Toronto, with various shots featuring city landmark buildings such as the Metropolitan United Church and Osgoode Hall.

Videodrome, 1983. David Cronenberg's classic science-fiction horror flick set in Toronto during the early 1980s.

Last Night, 1998. Torontonian Don McKellar directed this comedy drama, set and filmed in the city, about a group of people each facing the end of the world.

Owning Mahowny, 2003. Based on the true story of a Toronto bank manager who committed the largest bank fraud in Canadian history to feed his growing gambling habits.

Chloe, 2009. Toronto plays itself here in this well-received erotic thriller, also by Atom Egoyan. The Allan Gardens, the Royal Ontario Museum, the CN Tower, and other recognizable sites around the city are easily seen throughout the movie.

Scott Pilgrim vs. the World, 2010. Based on a graphic novel series, this action comedy, entirely filmed in Toronto, is about a young musician who must battle seven evil exes of his new girlfriend.

This Movie is Broken, 2010. A romantic comedy, set in Toronto, about a man attempting to win the heart of his long-time crush by taking her to a concert at the Harbourfront Centre.

Take This Waltz, 2011. A drama about a writer who lives in Toronto's Little Portugal neighborhood, and her relationships, both old and new.

ABOUT THIS BOOK

This *Explore Guide* has been produced by the editors of Insight Guides, whose books have set the standard for visual travel guides since 1970. With top-quality photography and authoritative recommendations, these guidebooks bring you the very best routes and itineraries in the world's most exciting destinations.

BEST ROUTES

The routes in the book provide something to suit all budgets, tastes and trip lengths. As well as covering the destination's many classic attractions, the itineraries track lesser-known sights, and there are also excursions for those who want to extend their visit outside the city. The routes embrace a range of interests, so whether you are an art fan, a gourmet, a history buff or have kids to entertain, you will find an option to suit.

We recommend reading the whole of a route before setting out. This should help you to familiarise yourself with it and enable you to plan where to stop for refreshments – options are shown in the 'Food and Drink' box at the end of each tour.

For our pick of the tours by theme, consult Recommended Routes for... (see pages 6–7).

INTRODUCTION

The routes are set in context by this introductory section, giving an overview of the destination to set the scene, plus background information on food and drink, shopping and more, while a succinct history timeline highlights the key events over the centuries.

DIRECTORY

Also supporting the routes is a Directory chapter, with a clearly organised A–Z of practical information, our pick of where to stay while you are there and select restaurant listings; these eateries complement the more low-key cafés and restaurants that feature within the routes and are intended to offer a wider choice for evening dining. Also included here are some nightlife listings and our recommendations for books and films about the destination.

ABOUT THE AUTHOR

After graduating with a degree in Anthropology, Lisa Voormeij, who's originally from The Netherlands, began working in IT development in West Africa. Fueled with exciting adventures, this lead to her launching her travel writing career. When she's not on location for work, she resides in the West Kootenay area of British Columbia with her two daughters, surrounded by the serenity of glacial lakes, alpine forests, and towering mountains.

CONTACT THE EDITORS

We hope you find this Explore Guide useful, interesting and a pleasure to read. If you have any questions or feedback on the text, pictures or maps, please do let us know. If you have noticed any errors or outdated facts, or have suggestions for places to include on the routes, we would be delighted to hear from you. Please drop us an email at hello@insightguides.com. Thanks!

CREDITS

Explore Toronto
Editor: Carine Tracanelli
Author: Lisa Voormeij
Head of DTP and Pre-Press: Rebeka Davies
Picture Editor: Michelle Bhatia
Cartography: original cartography Carte
Photo credits: Alamy 22, 24, 25T, 26, 27, 34, 35, 47, 51, 68T, 76T, 90, 99L, 107, 109, 121; Campbell House Museum 48B; Chuck Ortiz 92; Getty Images 65L, 98, 101, 104, 105L, 104/105, 114; Christophe Jivraj 96; Igor Yu 85; iStock 13, 14, 49, 50, 52B, 56, 111; Jake Kivanc 94; James Kachan Photography and Design 82/83; Jenna Marie Wakani 97L; Jesse Milns/Tourism Toronto 19, 28/29, 102, 116; Kayla Rocca 17; Khristel Stecher/Tourism Toronto 6TL, 66, 112B, 117, 119; Leonardo 86, 88B; Lisa Petrole 88T; Lisa Sakulensky Photography 33; Nick Merzetti 96/97; Olive Photography 89; Shutterstock 4/5, 6MC, 6ML, 6BC, 7T, 7MR, 7M, 7MR, 10, 11, 12, 15, 16, 18, 21B, 21T, 23, 25B, 30, 31, 32, 36, 37, 38, 39, 40, 41, 42, 43, 44B, 44T, 45, 46, 48T, 52T, 54B, 54T, 55, 57, 58B, 58T, 59, 60, 61, 62, 63, 64, 64/65, 67, 69L, 68/69, 70, 71, 72, 73, 74, 75L, 74/75, 77T, 78, 79, 80, 81, 84, 106, 108, 110, 112T, 113, 115, 118B, 118T, 120; Stacey Brandford 93; Stuart Sakai 98/99; Tide & Vine 100; Tony Lanz 68B; Tourism Toronto 20, 53, 76B, 77B, 87; Vintage Hotels 91; www.tedchaiphotography.com 95; Zach Slootsky 103
Cover credits: Getty Images (main) iStock (bottom)

Printed by CTPS – China
All Rights Reserved
© 2019 Apa Digital (CH) AG and
Apa Publications (UK) Ltd

First edition 2019

DISTRIBUTION

UK, Ireland and Europe
Apa Publications (UK) Ltd
sales@insightguides.com
United States and Canada
Ingram Publisher Services
ips@ingramcontent.com
Australia and New Zealand
Woodslane
info@woodslane.com.au
Southeast Asia
Apa Publications (Singapore) Pte
singaporeoffice@insightguides.com
Worldwide
Apa Publications (UK) Ltd
sales@insightguides.com

SPECIAL SALES, CONTENT LICENSING AND COPUBLISHING

Insight Guides can be purchased in bulk quantities at discounted prices. We can create special editions, personalised jackets and corporate imprints tailored to your needs.
sales@insightguides.com
www.insightguides.biz

INDEX

MAP LEGEND

- ● Start of tour
- → Tour & route direction
- ❶ Recommended sight
- ❷ Recommended restaurant/café
- ★ Place of interest
- ❶ Tourist information
- ✈ ✈ Airport / Airfield

- Ⓜ Subway station
- – – · Ferry route
- 🚌 Main bus station
- 𝗠̂ Museum
- 👤 Statue/monument
- ✚ Church
- ☪ Mosque
- 📖 Library
- 🎭 Theatre

- ✉ Main post office
- ⊕ Hospital
- 🗼 Lighthouse
- ⚲ Beach
-      Park
-      Important building
-      Urban area
-      Transport hub
-      National park

INSIGHT ⦿ GUIDES

OFF THE S

Since 1970, INSIGHT GUIDES has pro
the world's best travel destinations b
photography and illuminating text w

Whether you're planning a city break, a
lifetime, our superb range of guidebook
to discover more about your chosen des

INSIGHT GUIDES

offer a unique combination of stunning photos, absorbing narrative and detailed maps, providing all the inspiration and information you need.

PHRASEBOOKS & DICTIONARIES

help users to feel at home, when away. Pocket-sized with a free app to download, they go where you do.

CITY GUIDES

pack hundreds of great photos into a smaller format with detailed practical information, so you can navigate the world's top cities with confidence.

EXPLORE GUIDES

feature easy-to-follow walks and itineraries in the world's most exciting destinations, with our choice of the best places to eat and drink along the way.

POCKET GUIDES

combine concise information on where to go and what to do in a handy compact format, ideal on the ground. Includes a full-colour, fold-out map.

EXPERIENCE GUIDES

feature offbeat perspectives and secret gems for experienced travellers, with a collection of over 100 ideas for a memorable stay in a city.

www.insightguides.com